THE TOP 20 PASSAGES IN THE BIBLE

The Twenty Most Popular Passages From The Best-Selling Book Of All Time

ERIC ELDER

ACKNOWLEDGMENTS

Special thanks to my wife, Lana, who carefully read and revised each of these devotionals, infusing them with additional spiritual insights and practical wisdom.

Introduction

THE TOP 20 PASSAGES IN THE BIBLE

Scripture Reading: 2 Timothy 3:16-17

The Bible is the most quoted book in the world. Why? Maybe it's because the Bible has been around so long. Or maybe it's because the Bible is so big. But most likely it's because the Bible contains wisdom that has touched the lives of so many people throughout the ages and throughout the world.

When I saw a list one day of the top 20 passages in the Bible—those passages in the Bible that people turn to again and again, more frequently than any others—I was intrigued. I wondered, *What makes these passages so special? Are they words of comfort or words of conviction? Words of encouragement or words of challenge? Words of utter simplicity or words of profound depth?*

As I've looked through these passages, I've seen that they contain elements of all of these things. And I know from personal experience, having read each chapter many times over the years and at different stages of my life, that they contain some of the most inspiring, convicting, encouraging, and faith-building passages I've ever encountered. I can see why they have bubbled up to the top 20 passages of the Bible.

In the weeks ahead, I'd like to explore each of these top 20 passages with you as well, starting with number 20—the Christmas story from Luke chapter 1—and working our way to number 1, which just might surprise you!

Whether you've been an avid Bible reader for years, or you're brand new to discovering the life-changing power of its words, I think you'll truly enjoy this study—not just for the insights you'll learn about the passages, but because I believe that each passage can speak directly to your heart.

To be honest, I believe any passage from the Bible could speak to you just as profoundly. I couldn't count how many times I've had something on my mind and opened the Bible, only to find that God had something to say to me about it on the words on the pages before me.

How does God do this? I believe it's because the Word of God is "living and active," as it says in Hebrews 4:12 God has inspired the words on the pages by instilling them with His Spirit, and it is that same Spirit that brings them to life for you. All Scripture is literally "God-breathed," as it says in 2 Timothy 3:16.

So whether you turn to a top 20 passage or to one of the less celebrated ones, know that God can speak to you through His Word, if your heart is open to hearing from Him. No wonder the Bible is the best-selling, most translated, and most quoted book in the world!

I want to encourage you to pick up your Bible again today and read through it, praying as you go, and listening for God to speak. There's no doubt in my mind that the God who created you has things He'd love to speak to you, and things that you won't want to wait to hear.

Then join me in the pages ahead as we look at the top 20 passages from the Bible that people turn to again and again. I'm certain that God has things He wants you to know, things He wants you to do, and mysteries He wants to reveal.

P.S. As we go through this series, I'll also include a prayer and a memory verse from the passage we're studying, to encourage you in your personal prayer time with God, and to have something to memorize as we go along. Hiding God's Word in your heart is one of the best ways to recall it later when God wants to remind you of it. Here's today's prayer and memory verse...

PRAYER

Father, thank You for giving us Your words in the form of the Bible. Speak to us as we read from it today and in the days ahead, just as You spoke to those who first recorded these words for us to hear. In Jesus' name, Amen.

MEMORY VERSE

"All Scripture is breathed out by God and profitable for teaching, for reproof, for correction, and for training in righteousness, that the man of God may be competent, equipped for every good work" (1 Timothy 3:16-17, ESV).

THE CHRISTMAS STORY

Scripture Reading: Luke 1

We're looking at the Top 20 passages in the Bible—those chapters that people turn to again and again for God's wisdom—and we're starting today with number 20, the beginning of the Christmas story from Luke chapter 1 (it continues in chapter 2).

When you read Luke 1, you can see that it is filled with all the wonders of Christmas—miracles, angels, signs, and wonders—yet it was written by a man who was well-grounded in reality. Luke was a medical doctor, as noted by the Apostle Paul in Colossians 4:14, who set out to write an "orderly account" of the life of Christ for his friend Theophilus. Luke wrote:

"It seemed good to me also, having followed all things closely for some time past, to write an orderly account for you, most excellent Theophilus, that you may have certainty concerning the things you have been taught" (Luke 1:3-4).

Luke had carefully investigated these stories and had personally interviewed eyewitnesses of the accounts. He had traveled with Paul on his missionary journeys, and later documented their travels in the book of Acts.

Yet with all of Luke's detailed research and careful thought that he put into all of his writings, he still had room in his heart to try to convey—and not shy away from—the truly miraculous events that surrounded the birth of Christ and the events that followed throughout His life.

As a medical doctor, Luke—of all people —would have understood that it was nothing short of miraculous for Mary to give birth to a Son, even though she had never lain with a man. Yet Luke, of the four writers of the life of Christ (Matthew, Mark, Luke, and John), includes more details about Christ's birth than any of the others.

Perhaps it was precisely *because of* his experience as a doctor that Luke includes the miraculous aspects of this story. Having likely witnessed many births himself—as I have with my own six children—he would have known that every birth is a miracle from the hand of

God. So it would have been no stretch of the imagination for him to see that the miraculous events surrounding Christ's birth were from the hand of God as well.

Luke 1 also contains one of the most encouraging verses in all of Scripture about the power of God. It comes after the angel Gabriel announces to Mary that she's going to have a child. When Mary asks how this will happen, Gabriel says,

> *"The Holy Spirit will come upon you, and the power of the Most High will overshadow you. So the Holy One to be born will be called the Son of God. Even Elizabeth your relative is going to have a child in her old age, and she who was said to be barren is in her sixth month. For nothing is impossible with God" (Luke 1:35-37).*

And Gabriel would know. This is the same Gabriel who appeared to the prophet Daniel about 500 years earlier, revealing to him the exact timing of the Messiah's birth (see Daniel 9:21-27). And this is the same Gabriel who appeared to Elizabeth's husband, Zechariah, telling him that his wife would soon become pregnant. When Zechariah doubted, Gabriel said,

"I am Gabriel. I stand in the presence of God, and I have been sent to speak to you and to tell you this good news" (Luke 1:19).

It's as if Gabriel was saying, "Maybe you don't realize who I am...but I'm Gabriel, and I stand in the presence of God. Believe me when I say that when God makes a promise, He will fulfill it!"

Just as God fulfilled His promises to Zechariah and Elizabeth, to Joseph and Mary, to Daniel and a host of others in the Bible, God will fulfill His promises to you, too. Whatever you're facing, know that God can work miracles in your life. Nothing is impossible with Him. He can do anything!

He can restore your marriage, heal your sickness, bring you out of your financial troubles. He can restore relationships that are troubled in your life, He can find a new job for you that fits your giftings, He can even bring that child into your life that you've been longing for. Know that God will do whatever's best for you in every situation, but never doubt His miraculous power.

Read Luke chapter 1 for yourself and realize that nothing is impossible with God. Then put your faith in Him again today for everything in your life—even for those things which may seem impossible in your eyes.

PRAYER

Father, thank You for inspiring Luke to take the time to carefully investigate and document the miraculous life of Christ so that we, too, would know the certainty of what we have been taught. Lord, fill us with faith again today so that we can truly believe in our hearts that nothing is impossible with You. In Jesus' name, Amen.

MEMORY VERSE

"For nothing is impossible with God" (Luke 1:37).

Making The Best Use Of The Time

Scripture Reading: Ephesians 5

How do you make the best use of the time God has given you here on earth? That's what we're going to learn today as we look at Ephesians chapter 5 —the 19th most frequently read of the top 20 passages in the Bible.

When Billy Graham was asked what surprised him most about life, he responded, "The brevity of it."

Life is short, and God wants you to make the best use of the time that He's given you here on earth. He doesn't want you to waste it on sinful activities that, while possibly providing some momentary pleasure, will eventually end up wasting—and even destroying—your life and the lives of others.

In Paul's letter to the Ephesians, Paul writes:

"Look carefully then how you walk, not as unwise

but as wise, making the best use of the time, because the days are evil" (Ephesians 5:15-16).

There are a lot of ways you can spend your days, and Paul takes the rest of chapter 5 to compare and contrast several of them with practical examples. Here are a few:

In talking about living a life of purity, Paul says:

"Be imitators of God. And walk in love, as Christ loved us and gave Himself up for us...." (Ephesians 5:1-2a).

He goes on to say that we shouldn't have even a hint of sexual immorality, impurity, or covetousness, and adds:

"Let there be no filthiness nor foolish talk nor crude joking, which are out of place, but instead let there be thanksgiving" (Ephesians 5:3-4).

In talking about drinking, Paul says:

"And do not get drunk with wine, for that is debauchery, but be filled with the Spirit, addressing one another in psalms and hymns and spiritual

songs, singing and making melody to the Lord with your heart, giving thanks always and for everything to God the Father in the name of our Lord Jesus Christ" (Ephesians 5:18-20a).

In talking about relationships, Paul says not to abuse any authority God may have given you—whether it's between husbands and wives, children and parents, or workers and bosses—but to submit to one another out of love, being willing to give up your life for those God has put in your care, as Christ laid down His life for us (see Ephesians 5:22-33 and 6:1-9).

What do you want to be remembered for in life? And how might God want you to use your life to make a mark on this world for Him?

You may have heard of the famous Nobel Peace Prize, named after Alfred Nobel. But you may not have heard that Alfred Nobel was one of the wealthiest arms and weapons manufacturers in the world. When Alfred's brother died, a French newspaper mistakenly printed an obituary of Alfred instead, with the heading, "The merchant of death is dead." The paper went on to say that, "Dr. Alfred

Nobel, who became rich by finding ways to kill more people faster than ever before, died yesterday."

Alfred was so disturbed by this assessment of his life that he decided to change the way he lived it—and the way he would be remembered throughout history. He donated the bulk of his estate to establish the Nobel Prizes, given annually to those who have made an outstanding contribution to the world in the areas of physical science, chemistry, medical science, literature, and finally "peace." This man who might have been remembered as one of the most notorious "merchants of death" is now remembered as one of the most famous encouragers of peace.

Henry Manning, a priest back in 1884 wrote:

"Next to grace, time is the most precious gift of God. Yet how much of both we waste."

God doesn't want you to waste the days He's given you. He wants you to make the best of them. If you're not sure how to do that, read Ephesians 5 and look for specific things that God might want you to start—or stop—doing in your life. Then do what Paul encouraged the Ephesians to do:

> *"Look carefully then how you walk...making the best use of the time..."*

PRAYER

> *Father, thank You for giving us the time we have here on the earth. Help us to make the best use of time that we can. Keep us from destroying ourselves and others by the things we think and say and do, and help us to bless You and bless others instead. In Jesus' name, Amen.*

MEMORY VERSE

> *"Look carefully then how you walk, not as unwise but as wise, making the best use of the time, because the days are evil" (Ephesians 5:15-16, ESV).*

God's Love For You

Scripture Reading: Ephesians 1

One of the most difficult things in life is to grasp God's incredible love for you. Your view of His love may be impaired because of difficult circumstances you're facing, or particular sins—whether past or present, or because of poor examples of how a loving Father acts and behaves based on some faulty earthly models, or for a hundred other reasons.

If any of these are the case for you, I'd encourage you to take a close look at chapter 1 of Ephesians (and chapters 2 and 3 if you can), asking God as you read to open the eyes of your heart to His great love.

Paul felt so passionately about this topic that he spent the first half of his letter to the Ephesians telling them of God's great love for them—and the grace that God was eager to extend to them in Christ.

In chapter 1, he prays for them that God:

"...may give you a spirit of wisdom and of revela-

tion in the knowledge of Him, having the eyes of your hearts enlightened, that you may know what is the hope to which He has called you, what are the riches of His glorious inheritance in the saints, and what is the immeasurable greatness of His power toward us who believe..." (Ephesians 1:17b-19a).

In chapter 2, he says,

"For by grace you have been saved through faith. And this is not your own doing; it is the gift of God, not a result of works, so that no one may boast. For we are His workmanship, created in Christ Jesus for good works, which God prepared beforehand, that we should walk in them" (Ephesians 2:8-10).

And in chapter 3, he prays,

"...that you, being rooted and grounded in love, may have strength to comprehend with all the saints what is the breadth and length and height and depth, and to know the love of Christ that surpasses knowledge, that you may be filled with all the fullness of God" (Ephesians 3:17b-19).

God loves you deeply, yet grasping it can be one of the hardest things you'll ever do in your life. But grasping it will also bring you more joy than you've ever known in your life.

Paul seems to have discovered what it meant—at the deepest level—to be "adopted" by God. While some who are adopted find it hard to get over their feelings of abandonment, others realize that being adopted means that that they don't belong to someone by chance, but by choice. Paul clearly had this latter view, as he reminded the Ephesians:

"In love He predestined us for adoption as sons through Jesus Christ, according to the purpose of His will, to the praise of His glorious grace, with which He has blessed us in the Beloved" (Ephesians 1:5-6).

Mother Teresa, who took in and cared for thousands of children during her lifetime, seemed to capture the heart of God towards those who feel "unwanted" in a beautiful way when she said,

"There is no such thing as an unwanted child. If

you don't want them, give them to me. I want them."

God feels the same way about you. Although you may feel like others have abandoned you, God never has. He *has* always loved you, *will* always love you, and *still* loves you today as much as He ever has. Why? Because you are His beloved child. You are made in His image. You are His own precious creation. He loves you deeply and wants more than anything in the world to have an intimate relationship with you.

If I could do one thing for you today, it would be to do what the Apostle Paul did for the Ephesians: to get down on my knees and pray that God would open the eyes of your heart, and that you would be able to comprehend the breadth and length and height and depth of God's love for you in Christ. And that's just what I'm going to do in my prayer here.

PRAYER

Father, I pray that every person reading these words would be able to grasp Your incredible love for them in a deeper way than ever before. Open the eyes of their heart, that they would be able to comprehend the breadth and length and height and depth of God's love for them in Christ. In Jesus' name, Amen.

MEMORY VERSE

"In love He predestined us for adoption as sons through Jesus Christ, according to the purpose of His will, to the praise of His glorious grace, with which He has blessed us in the Beloved" (Ephesians 1:5-6).

THE GOSPEL IN A NUTSHELL

Scripture Reading: John 3

I f you were to look at a list of the top 100 verses in the Bible, you'd find a verse from John chapter 3 at the very top. It's the most quoted verse in the Bible, and the most quoted verse of Jesus. Speaking of Himself, Jesus said:

> *"For God so loved the world, that He gave His only Son, that whoever believes in Him should not perish but have eternal life" (John 3:16).*

John 3:16 contains the gospel in a nutshell, the good news of Jesus in compact form: that if anyone who wants to be free from the penalty of sin and death, they can do so by putting their faith in Jesus.

Jesus expanded on why this is such good news in the rest of John 3. He did so in the context of a conversation that took place between Himself and Nicodemus, a member of the Jewish ruling council, who came to Je-

sus one night to learn more from this contro-
versial, but impressive, teacher.

Jesus told Nicodemus: "You must be born
again," to which Nicodemus responded:

*"How can a man be born when he is old? Can he
enter a second time into his mother's womb and be
born?" (John 3:4).*

Jesus answered him:

*"Truly, truly, I say to you, unless one is born of
water and the Spirit, he cannot enter the kingdom
of God" (John 3:5).*

Nicodemus must have taken what Jesus
said to heart, for after Jesus died on the cross,
Nicodemus, along with Joseph of Arimathea,
risked his life and position on the Jewish
council by asking Pilate for Jesus' body in order to give Jesus a proper burial (see John
19:38-40). May God give us all that kind of
boldness in our faith!

Jesus also mentioned in his conversation
with Nicodemus something significant that
had happened to the Israelites about 2,500
years earlier. When the Israelites were wan-

dering in the desert, they sinned. As a result, God sent fiery serpents to attack them, and many Israelites died from the bites. Those who were still alive repented of their sins and Moses prayed to God on their behalf. God said to Moses:

> " *Make a fiery serpent and set it on a pole, and everyone who is bitten, when he sees it, shall live.' So Moses made a bronze serpent and set it on a pole. And if a serpent bit anyone, he would look at the bronze serpent and live"* (Numbers 21:8-9).

God heard their prayers and saw their repentant hearts and provided a way for them to be saved. Referring to this story, Jesus told Nicodemus:

> *"And as Moses lifted up the serpent in the wilderness, so must the Son of Man be lifted up, that whoever believes in Him may have eternal life"* (John 3:14-15).

This story has become such a symbol of healing that today, the symbol of a snake wrapped around a pole is still displayed on many of our medical buildings, ambulances, and doctor's insignias.

But it's more than just a symbol of healing. It's a symbol of forgiveness, a symbol of a loving God who will go to the great lengths to extend forgiveness to His people, if only they would turn from their sins and put their faith in Him.

It is in the context of this ancient story of God's forgiveness and healing that Jesus said His most famous quote in John 3:16:

"For God so loved the world, that He gave His only Son, that whoever believes in Him should not perish but have eternal life" (John 3:16).

I bring this up because John 3:16 is not only the gospel in a nutshell, it's *the whole Bible* in a nutshell! God has always been wooing His people into a relationship with Him, and offering them forgiveness if they truly desire it, so that they can come back into a relationship with Him. And that's what God has offered to us, by sending His only Son to die for us so we can live.

God loves you, and He doesn't want you or anyone else to be destroyed by sin. He's willing to go to the greatest lengths possible—and He already has—to see that you will be healed, forgiven, and brought back into a new life with Him.

If you've already put your faith in Christ, Hallelujah! Let someone know about it who needs to hear this good news! But if you've never put your faith in Christ—been "born again," to use Jesus' words—there's no better time than right now!

PRAYER

Father, thank You for loving me so much that You would send Your only Son to die for me so that I could live. I want to live again. I want to be born again spiritually so I can live with You forever. Forgive me for my sins, for the wrong things I've done. I am putting my faith in Christ right now. Fill me with Your Spirit so that I can live the life You've called me to live, both here on earth, and on into heaven forever. In Jesus' name, Amen.

MEMORY VERSE

"For God so loved the world, that He gave His

only Son, that whoever believes in Him should not perish but have eternal life" (John 3:16, ESV).

THE POWER OF GOD FOR SALVATION

Scripture Reading: Romans 1

If I had to choose one passage from the Bible that God has used most to change *my* life, it would be Romans chapter 1. It's not my favorite passage in the Bible, because Romans 1 is not particularly cheery or uplifting. In fact, it contains some of the worst news I've ever heard in my life!

But the truth is the gospel is often "bad news" before it's "good news." There's no reason to put your faith in a Savior unless you realize that there's something in your life from which you need to be saved. And that was the case with me: I didn't realize there was anything in my life I needed saving from until I read Romans chapter 1. Then I realized that I, too, needed a Savior.

The book of Romans is actually a letter that the Apostle Paul wrote to the believers who lived in Rome. Paul longed to see them so they could mutually encourage one another in their faith, and so he could reap a harvest among them, bringing still more people to faith in Christ. He loved preaching about Christ, even though it had landed him in prison many times. He said:

"For I am not ashamed of the gospel, for it is the power of God for salvation to everyone who believes, to the Jew first and also to the Greek" (Romans 1:16).

Paul then began to describe the gospel that he loved to preach, starting with the "bad news" that God was revealing His wrath from heaven against all ungodliness and unrighteousness.

As I read through Paul's words in chapter 1, I was struck by the fact that God's wrath wasn't so much that He was raining fire down from heaven, or causing calamity among the people. His wrath was quite simply this: giving people up to follow their own sinful desires and choices, and then letting the natural consequences of those choices overtake them.

Three times in Romans 1, Paul describes God's wrath in similar terms:

"Therefore God gave them up in the lusts of their hearts to impurity, to the dishonoring of their bodies among themselves..." (Romans 1:24).

"For this reason God gave them up to dishonorable passions..." (Romans 1:26a).

"And since they did not see fit to acknowledge God, God gave them up to a debased mind to do what ought not to be done..." (Romans 1:28).

As I read through this list of things that people did to dishonor God, I realized that I had done many of them myself. I had, as Paul described it so eloquently, "exchanged the truth about God for a lie" (Romans 1:25). And I, too, was "without excuse" (Romans 1:20b), for I knew in my heart that what I was doing was wrong, if only from the evidence of the natural order of God's creation itself.

It was the worst news I had ever heard. I had sinned against God and His wrath was now bearing down heavily upon me, a wrath that threatened to manifest itself in ways that were simply the natural result of the sinful choices I had made.

That's when I finally realized the "good

news" of the gospel: that God already knew about my sins and had sent His Son to save me from them, if I would put my faith in Him.

Within 24 hours of reading Romans chapter 1, I decided to put my faith in Christ for everything in my life. I asked Him to forgive me of my sins and to fill me with His Holy Spirit so I could live the life He wanted me to live. He did exactly what He promised and I'm now on a new path, a path of life that leads on into eternity.

The whole book of Romans is incredibly thought-provoking, and we'll revisit some more passages from it later in this series. I hope you'll take a chance to read through all of Romans yourself, starting with chapter 1, inviting God to speak to you as you read. It's turned me into a *believer,* and it's *saved* me—just as Paul said it would. The gospel of Jesus Christ really is, "the power of God for salvation to everyone who believes..."

Prayer

Father, thank You for loving us enough to give us the free will to choose Your path or choose our own.

But Father, we pray that You would fill us with Your Spirit again today so that we will always choose to follow You in everything we do, avoiding the wrath that we would otherwise bring upon ourselves. We put our faith in Christ again today for everything in our lives. In Jesus' name, Amen.

MEMORY VERSE

"For I am not ashamed of the gospel, for it is the power of God for salvation to everyone who believes, to the Jew first and also to the Greek" (Romans 1:16, ESV).

WALKING IN A MANNER WORTHY OF YOUR CALLING

Scripture Reading: Ephesians 4

One of the benefits of reading the Bible is that it acts as a counselor of sorts, giving you advice on how to handle the situations you face in life. In fact, the Holy Spirit is often called *the Counselor,* and He does some of His best counseling work as you read through the pages of the Bible.

Ephesians 4 is one of those passages that can help you in various ways, including when you're feeling frustrated or angry with those around you. God knows what you're feeling, and so does the Apostle Paul, who wrote the letter to the Ephesians.

Having been unjustly imprisoned for his faith, Paul could have easily given in to the temptation to be bitter and angry with those around him. But instead he chose another path—and he encouraged the Ephesians to do the same:

"I therefore, a prisoner for the Lord, urge you to walk in a manner worthy of the calling to which you have been called, with all humility and gentleness, with patience, bearing with one another in love, eager to maintain the unity of the Spirit in the bond of peace" (Ephesians 4:1-3).

How could Paul do it? How could he turn off the anger that might otherwise have boiled up within him—and perhaps even consumed him? To answer that question, I think we need to look closer at the little word he uses at the beginning of the chapter: "therefore." Whenever you see a "therefore" in the Bible, it's a good idea to read the words leading up to it so you'll know what the "therefore" is there for!

If you look back at what Paul was writing prior to this chapter, you'll see that he spent the entire first three chapters of the book trying to help the Ephesians understand just how much God really loved them. He even got down on his knees and prayed for them to understand the depth of God's love. Paul knew that once they understood God's unconditional love for them, then they would be able to extend that same love to those around them.

35

There's a "Dennis the Menace" cartoon in which Dennis and his friend Joey are walking away from the Wilson's house with their hands full of cookies. Joey asks, "I wonder what we did to deserve this?"

Dennis tells his friend, "Joey, Mrs. Wilson gives us cookies not because *we're* nice, but because *she's* nice."

The same can be said of God. The reason He treats us with so much love and kindness is not necessarily because *we're* good, but because *He's* good. That's how Paul was able to treat others with kindness even though they were mistreating him, and that's how we can treat others with kindness even though they may be mistreating us.

Paul was able to "be nice" to them because God had "been nice" to him. As Paul renewed his mind with this reminder of God's love, he was able to extend that love to others, regardless of how they treated him. Paul told the Ephesians:

"...to put off your old self, which belongs to your former manner of life and is corrupt through deceitful desires, and to be renewed in the spirit of your minds, and to put on the new self, created

after the likeness of God in true righteousness and holiness" (Ephesians 4:17-24).

If you're struggling to love those around you with the love that God has expressed to you, I'd encourage you to read through all of Ephesians chapter 4 (and keep on reading, if you'd like, through chapters 5 and 6 as well!) You'll find some of the most practical words of advice from the best Counselor in the world. Here are just a few of His pieces of wisdom:

"Be angry and do not sin; do not let the sun go down on your anger, and give no opportunity to the devil" (Ephesians 4:26-27).

"Let no corrupting talk come out of your mouths, but only such as is good for building up, as fits the occasion, that it may give grace to those who hear" (Ephesians 4:29).

"Be kind to one another, tenderhearted, forgiving one another, as God in Christ forgave you" (Ephesians 4:32).

These aren't generic platitudes; they're life-changing attitudes—attitudes that will change how you act.

As a Christian, God has put a great calling on your life. Invite God to renew Your mind, and then do as Paul urged the Ephesians to do:

"...to walk in a manner worthy of the calling to which you have been called, with all humility and gentleness, with patience, bearing with one another in love, eager to maintain the unity of the Spirit in the bond of peace."

PRAYER

Father, thank You for Your incredible love for us. Help us to understand just how wide and long and high and deep it is, so that we can extend that love to those around us. Help us to walk in a manner worthy of the calling that You have put upon our lives, and may our walk impact those around us in powerful ways as well. In Jesus' name, Amen.

MEMORY VERSE

"I therefore, a prisoner for the Lord, urge you to walk in a manner worthy of the calling to which

*you have been called, with all humility and gentle-
ness, with patience, bearing with one another in
love, eager to maintain the unity of the Spirit in
the bond of peace" (Ephesians 4:1-3).*

GOD KNOWS YOU

Scripture Reading: Psalm 139

I f you've ever wondered if God knows what you're going through—if He can see into your heart and know what you're thinking and feeling and experiencing in your life, then you'll want to read Psalm 139.

The word "psalm" means "song,"—or a poem set to music—so the book of Psalms is the songbook of the Bible. Although the tunes aren't recorded for us, the words themselves sing of the wonders of God. And in Psalm 139, they sing of just how deeply God knows each one of us—including you.

Even though this song was written by King David about 3,000 years ago, you can still hear God's voice to you today as you read his opening words. Listen to hear just how deeply God knows you and knows what you're going through in your life.

"O LORD, You have searched me and known me!

You know when I sit down and when I rise up;

You discern my thoughts from afar.
You search out my path and my lying down
   and are acquainted with all my ways.
Even before a word is on my tongue,
   behold, O LORD, You know it altogether.
You hem me in, behind and before,
   and lay Your hand upon me.
Such knowledge is too wonderful for me;
   it is high; I cannot attain it.
Where shall I go from Your Spirit?
   Or where shall I flee from Your presence?
If I ascend to heaven, You are there!
   If I make my bed in Sheol, You are there!
If I take the wings of the morning
   and dwell in the uttermost parts of the sea,
even there Your hand shall lead me,
   and Your right hand shall hold me."
   (Psalm 139:1-10)

These words are especially meaningful to me today as I'm headed to the airport as I write this. I'm sending my son off to college in Sydney, Australia, and my daughter off to college in Lynchburg, Virginia. What a joy and comfort to know that God will be going with both of them as they "take the wings of the morning" and fly so far from home, even dwelling in "the uttermost parts of the sea!"

Just as I know from Psalm 139 that God is with me and will be with my kids wherever they go, I also know that God is with you and will be with your loved ones wherever they go. For there's no place in the world that you can go where God is *not* there!

As David went on to say in Psalm 139:

"If I say, 'Surely the darkness shall cover me,
and the light about me be night,'
even the darkness is not dark to You;
the night is bright as the day,
for darkness is as light with You."
(Psalm 139:11-12)

Even if it looks dark all around you, know that God is still right there with you. The darkness doesn't matter to Him. In His eyes, "the night is as bright as the day." You're not alone. God loves you. He sees you. And He knows what you're going through.

I can say this with confidence because no one knows you better than Him. He created you. He saw what you looked like before any-one else did, while He was still forming you in your mother's womb. And even before you lived a single day of your life, God had a plan for every one of them.

As David sang:

"For You formed my inward parts;
  You knitted me together in my mother's womb.
I praise You, for I am fearfully and wonderfully made.
  Wonderful are Your works;
  my soul knows it very well.
My frame was not hidden from You,
  when I was being made in secret,
  intricately woven in the depths of the earth.
Your eyes saw my unformed substance;
  in Your book were written, every one of them,
  the days that were formed for me,
  when as yet there was none of them."
  (Psalm 139:13-16)

God knows you. He loves you. And He has an incredible purpose for your life, just as He knows and loves and has an incredible purpose for the lives of every one you know. Read all of Psalm 139 today, and let the truth of God's words sink deep into your heart.

PRAYER

Father, thank You for the reminder today of how great Your love is for each one of us. Thank You that there's nothing hidden from You and that there's no place we can go where You aren't there with us. In Jesus' name, Amen.

MEMORY VERSE:

"O LORD, You have searched me and known me! You know when I sit down and when I rise up; You discern my thoughts from afar" (Psalm 139:1, ESV).

Number 13

LIKE A TREE PLANTED BY WATER

Scripture Reading: Psalm 1

Several years ago I was praying about what I could do with my life for God. I wanted to serve Him in some great way, and was willing to go wherever He wanted me to go and do whatever He wanted me to do.

One day a friend of mine was praying for me. As he prayed, he said he saw me as if I were a tree, not necessarily going or doing anything at all, but standing still and growing tall. He said that as I grew, people would come and rest under the shade of my branches.

It was a great picture, but it wasn't quite what I had in mind. I wanted to go and do something spectacular for God, but it sounded like God wanted me to stay where I was and keep growing in Him. It reminded me in a way of the passage that we're looking at today, Psalm 1. It's a passage that describes just such a man:

*"He is like a tree
   planted by streams of water
   that yields its fruit in its season,
   and its leaf does not wither.
   In all that he does, he prospers."
   (Psalm 1:2)*

As I read that passage, all of a sudden, it didn't sound so bad to me. How awesome it would be to be like a tree planted by streams of water. To dig my roots deep into the ground and soak up all I could of the life-giving water nearby. To be able to yield fruit when it was time. To know that my leaves would never wither. And to know that in all I did I would prosper.

I wanted to be like that tree, so I looked at the rest of Psalm 1 where it showed me how:

*"Blessed is the man
   who walks not in the counsel of the wicked,
   nor stands in the way of sinners,
   nor sits in the seat of scoffers;
   but his delight is in the law of the LORD,
   and on His law he meditates day and night"
   (Psalm 1:1-2)*

Rather than entering into the ways of the wicked and sinners and scoffers, God wanted me to dig deep into His Word—to take delight in reading it and meditating on it day and night. In the process, I would grow stronger and taller in my faith and in my life. And as I grew, I would be blessed and so would those around me, as a natural byproduct of my own growth.

I felt both relief and exhilaration at the same time. Instead of having to try to figure everything out right away, I could focus simply on meditating on God's Word, letting God bring the fruit "in its season."

There's something spectacular about reading and meditating on God's Word. A monk named Thomas Merton said:

> *"By reading the scriptures I am so renewed that all nature seems renewed around me and with me. The sky seems to be a pure, a cooler blue, the trees a deeper green. The whole world is charged with the glory of God and I feel fire and music under my feet."*

If you want to serve God in a powerful

way, I encourage you to take the words of Psalm 1 to heart. Don't take the path of the wicked and sinners and scoffers. Take the path instead of meditating on God's Word day and night. Send your roots deep into His life-giving words. And as you and your faith grow, you will be blessed—and so will those around you. You'll have a new outlook on life, and others will gather around just to rest in the shade of your tree.

PRAYER

Father, thank You for giving us Your Word so that we can read it, meditate on it, and grow in our faith and in our lives. Help us to grow strong and tall as we read Your Word, so that we can bear fruit "in its season," blessing others along the way. In Jesus' name, Amen.

MEMORY VERSE

"Blessed is the man who walks not in the counsel of the wicked, nor stands in the way of sinners, nor sits in the seat of scoffers; but his delight is in the law of the LORD, and on His law he meditates day and night" (Psalm 1:1, ESV).

Don't Be Anxious

Scripture Reading: Philippians 4

I f you're feeling anxious or worried about anything today, Philippians 4 is a good place to look for help.

I like this passage because the Apostle Paul, who wrote these God-inspired words, doesn't just tell you *not* to be anxious, he tells you *why* you don't need to be anxious; he doesn't just tell you *not* to dwell on your problems, but he tells you *what* to dwell on instead.

And I especially like this passage because Paul didn't write these words while sitting on a grassy hillside at a mountaintop retreat. He wrote them while being held in chains in a first century prison cell, having been beaten, flogged, and facing possible death at any moment. If Paul could learn how to be free from anxiety in a situation like that, then we might be able to learn from him how to deal with our anxious thoughts as well.

Here's what Paul said:

"Rejoice in the Lord always; again I will say, Re-

joice. Let your reasonableness be known to everyone. The Lord is at hand; do not be anxious about anything, but in everything by prayer and supplication with thanksgiving let your requests be made known to God. And the peace of God, which surpasses all understanding, will guard your hearts and your minds in Christ Jesus" (Philippians 4:4-7).

Twice he says to "rejoice in the Lord."

Notice that he doesn't say you have to rejoice about the difficult situation your facing, but to rejoice *in the Lord.* Rather than trying to minimize what you're facing, Paul is trying to maximize who you're facing them with: the Lord.

That's also the reason *why* you don't need to be anxious—because "The Lord is at hand." He's not a God who has taken off to some distant land, but He's actually very close at all times—"at hand"—within an arm's reach.

A woman once told me about a time when she was laying in pain on a hospital bed when she looked up to see a cross on the wall. It wasn't an empty cross—which has a special significance of its own—but it was a cross depicting the agonizing crucifixion of Jesus.

While it might seem gruesome to look into the face of a man who is experiencing excruciating pain, for this woman it turned out to be one of the greatest comforts of her life. She was suddenly filled with the realization that Jesus was right there with her—that He knew exactly what she was going through— and He brought her immediate comfort and peace.

Paul also told the Philippians *what* to focus on in the midst of their troubles:

> *"Finally, brothers, whatever is true, whatever is honorable, whatever is just, whatever is pure, whatever is lovely, whatever is commendable, if there is any excellence, if there is anything worthy of praise, think about these things. What you have learned and received and heard and seen in me—practice these things, and the God of peace will be with you" (Philippians 4:8-9).*

It reminds me of the song that Julie Andrews sang in the Rodgers and Hammerstein musical, *The Sound of Music.* When the children were afraid of the thunder and lightning outside, she sang: "When the dog bites, when the bee stings, when I'm feeling sad, I simply remember my favorite things, and then I don't feel so bad." For her, some of her favorite things were, "Raindrops on roses and whiskers on kittens, bright copper kettles and warm woolen mittens."

What about you? What are some of your favorite things? Or, as Paul asked, what are some things you can think about that are true? Honorable? Just? Pure? Lovely? Commendable? Excellent? Worthy of praise? Think about such things—not just as a technique to distract you from your situation, but as a practical way to put your situation into perspective. For as hard as life can be, there are still things in life which are beautiful and glorious.

Paul learned the secret of being content in every situation, whether he had plenty or was in want. How? By continually *rejoicing in the Lord,* by remembering that *God is at hand,* and in everything, *making his requests known to God.* In one of the most famous verses of the Bible—found at the end of this chapter in Philippians—Paul said:

"I can do all things through Him who strengthens me" (Philippians 4:13).

If you're feeling anxious and worried today, read Philippians chapter 4. Learn from Paul and put into practice what you learn. As you do, may the God of peace be with you—and may *His* peace be yours.

PRAYER

Father, thank You for giving us practical ways to face the things that cause us to be anxious. Help us to remember that You are near, and to dwell on those things that are true, honorable, just, pure, lovely, commendable, excellent, and worthy of praise. In Jesus' name, Amen.

MEMORY VERSE

"Do not be anxious about anything, but in everything by prayer and supplication with thanksgiving let your requests be made known to God" (Philippians 4:6, ESV).

A LIVING SACRIFICE

Scripture Reading: Romans 12

What are some things that you feel passionate about—things that you like to do that bring joy to you and to those around you? Chances are, God has gifted you in a special way to do those very things. And when you do them, you bring joy to His heart as well.

A man named Eric Liddle loved God. He also loved to run. He wanted to spend his life as a missionary, but he also had a chance to run in the Olympic games. Torn between running or being a missionary, he eventually did both. As he told one of his friends: "When God created me, He made me fast, and when I run, I feel His pleasure."

God has created and gifted each one of us uniquely. To some He has given the gift of teaching, to others, serving, to still others, the gifts of leading or healing or giving or showing mercy. God wants you to use your gifts to the fullest. In Romans 12, the Apostle Paul talks about how you can do just that:

"I appeal to you therefore, brothers, by the mercies of God, to present your bodies as a living sacrifice, holy and acceptable to God, which is your spiritual worship. ... Having gifts that differ according to the grace given to us, let us use them: if prophecy, in proportion to our faith; if service, in our serving; the one who teaches, in his teaching; the one who exhorts, in his exhortation; the one who contributes, in generosity; the one who leads, with zeal; the one who does acts of mercy, with cheerfulness."
(Romans 12:1, 6-8)

The word sacrifice in this context comes from the Greek word "thusia," which means "to make an offering." A living sacrifice, then, is someone who "makes an offering" of their life to God. It's also the basis for our English word "enthusiasm," which means "infused with the Divine Spirit"—a passionate drive that has been given to us by God.

In the movie, *Amazing Grace,* you can see what this kind of passionate drive from God looks like in action. The movie tells the true story of William Wilberforce, a British man who "found God" while he was serving as a member of parliament. Wilberforce considered giving up his position in politics to go into pastoral ministry. But he also had a passion to abolish the slave trade in England, a passion which few people shared at the time, for slavery was firmly entrenched in the economy and culture of many English outposts.

Upon hearing that Wilberforce was facing such a dilemma, his good friend and soon-to-be prime minister of England, William Pitt, arranged a meeting between Wilberforce and some of the other passionate abolitionists. One of them, a pastor, said, "Mr. Wilberforce, we understand you're having problems choosing whether to do the work of God or the work of a political activist." Another added, quietly, "We humbly suggest that you can do both."

Rather than *leave* politics, Wilberforce spent the next thirty years as a member of parliament, using his God-given gifts of eloquence, wisdom, and faith to help bring about the end of slavery throughout the entire British Empire.

What about you? What kinds of gifts might God want you to use for Him? By thinking about those things which you feel most passionate about, it can help you identify what gifts God may most want to use within you.

Someone recently asked me, "If you could be the best in the world at one particular skill, what would it be, and why?" The first thing that came to my mind was "preaching," because I like the idea of being able interact and shape the lives of people God has brought into my life. But the second thing that came to my mind was "writing," because as much as I love personally interacting with people, I know that by writing down the thoughts and ideas that God is putting into my mind, I can influence people's lives for generations to come. Thinking about these two passions in my life has helped me to focus on those things that God has gifted me to do as well.

A Jesuit priest named John Powell talks of an old Christian tradition that says, "God sends every person into the world with a special message to deliver, with a special song to sing for others, and a special act of love to bestow. No one else can speak your message, or sing your song, or offer your act of love. These are entrusted only to you."

When you think about your own gifts, your own passions, your own special skills that you could use to "make an offering" to God, what comes to mind? What do you feel passionate about? How has God gifted or empowered you? How has He infused His Divine Spirit within you in a particular way?

If you're not sure what your spiritual gifts might be, read through some of the gifts God has poured out on his people as recorded in Romans 12, 1 Corinthians 12, and Ephesians 4 and try to identify some of those which you feel most passionate about.

If you put even one or two of these gifts into use in your own life this week, I think you'll find out even more what it means to be "a living sacrifice, holy and pleasing to God."

PRAYER

Father, thank You for giving us spiritual gifts, gifts that we can use to bless You and bless those around us. We pray that You would help us to understand our gifts even better, so that we can live our lives in such a way that we are truly "living sacrifices," holy and pleasing to You. In Jesus' name, Amen.

MEMORY VERSE

"I appeal to you therefore, brothers, by the mercies of God, to present your bodies as a living sacrifice, holy and acceptable to God, which is your spiritual worship" (Romans 12:1, ESV).

THE REALITY OF HEAVEN

Scripture Reading: John 14

I'd like to share a conversation I had with a man on a small plane in the Philippines. My wife and I were on a missions trip, flying between two of the islands, and an elderly man was seated next to us. His wife, unfortunately, had recently passed away.

When he found out we were on a missions trip, he asked us a very heartfelt question. He said that he missed his wife greatly, and wondered where she was now. He wanted to know if she was OK.

I asked him, "Was she a Christian? Did she believe in Jesus?"

He answered, "Yes, she was, and yes, she believed in Him very deeply."

I said, "Then let's take a look at what Jesus said about where she is now." Then I opened my Bible and read to him these words of Jesus from John chapter 14:

"Let not your hearts be troubled. Believe in God; believe also in Me. In My Father's house are many

rooms. If it were not so, would I have told you that I go to prepare a place for you? And if I go and prepare a place for you, I will come again and will take you to Myself, that where I am you may be also" (John 14:1-3).

As I read Jesus' words, the man began to weep. Suddenly, he knew where his wife was. He knew she was in heaven. · He knew she was with Jesus.

Jesus had many other things to say to His disciples in John chapter 14, just as He still has much to say to us today.

He assured them that even though He was going to heaven, He would still be able to hear their prayers. More than that, He assured them that He would answer them, if they asked for anything in His name:

"Whatever you ask in My name, this I will do, that the Father may be glorified in the Son. If you ask Me anything in My name, I will do it" (John 14:13-14).

And then, as you would expect from any good relationship, Jesus said that He had things He wanted them to do as well:

*"If you love Me, you will keep My command-
ments. ... If anyone loves Me, he will keep My
word, and My Father will love him, and we will
come to him and make our home with him. Whoever does not love Me does not keep My words.
And the word that you hear is not mine but the
Father's who sent Me." (John 14:15).*

He also assured them that He wasn't going
to leave them alone, because the Father was
going to send His Holy Spirit to them. He
said:

*"These things I have spoken to you while I am still
with you. But the Helper, the Holy Spirit, whom
the Father will send in My name, He will teach
you all things and bring to your remembrance all
that I have said to you. Peace I leave with you;
My peace I give to you. Not as the world gives do
I give to you. Let not your hearts be troubled,
neither let them be afraid" (John 14:18-20, 25-
27).*

There's a note I've seen that summarizes
the message of John 14 quite simply. It says:

"Gone to My Father's house to prepare a place for you. Be back soon - Love, Jesus"

You don't get to heaven by plane or train, by car or bus, or even by rocket ship. You get to heaven by putting your faith in Christ, and letting Him take you there Himself. As Jesus told His disciples, when they asked Him how to get there, He said:

"I am the way, and the truth, and the life. No one comes to the Father except through Me" (John 14:6).

If you need assurance today that heaven is real, that Jesus hears your prayers (and will answer them!), and that He has not left you here alone, I'd encourage you to read the rest of John 14 for yourself. Just as the man seated next to us on the plane in the Philippines found the answers to His questions in these words from Jesus, so can you.

PRAYER

Father, thank You for Your reassuring words that You've already gone ahead of us into heaven, and that You're preparing a place for us even now. Help us to continue to put our trust in You that we will be in heaven with you in forever, and continue to fill us with Your Holy Spirit, so that we can do all that You've called us to do here on earth. In Jesus' name, Amen.

MEMORY VERSE

"Let not your hearts be troubled. Believe in God; believe also in Me. In My Father's house are many rooms. If it were not so, would I have told you that I go to prepare a place for you?" (John 14:1, ESV).

NEED WISDOM? ASK GOD!

Scripture Reading: James 1

When people write to me asking for prayer about what to do in a particular situation, I'll often include in my reply a quote from James chapter 1. That's because James states clearly and emphatically that God loves to pour out His wisdom on those who ask for it.

And because people are facing so many decisions in their lives—whether it's in regards to their relationships, careers, health, finances, ministries, and so on—I find myself quoting James quite a bit. Here's what James says:

"If any of you lacks wisdom, let him ask God, who gives generously to all without reproach, and it will be given him" (James 1:5).

This is a simple, yet beautiful verse. It's simple, because it contains a very basic message: if you need wisdom, ask God. It's beautiful, because it gives you assurance that your prayers are not in vain, that God *will* give you His wisdom, generously and without reproach—meaning He will not rebuke you for asking. He knows that your wisdom is limited, and that's OK.

But believe it or not, as much as you might want to know God's will for your life, God wants you to know it even more. He has a vested interest in your decisions, and He is more than willing to help you make them—if you're willing to ask.

James goes on to say that the *way* you ask for wisdom will help to ensure that you'll receive it: he says to ask for it *in faith:*

"But let him ask in faith, with no doubting, for the one who doubts is like a wave of the sea that is driven and tossed by the wind. For that person must not suppose that he will receive anything from the Lord; he is a double-minded man, unstable in all his ways" (James 1:6-8).

God wants you to come to Him in faith, believing that He will answer you, and believing that His answer is truly the best for you. Some people come to God wanting to hear His thoughts on a matter first, *then* they decide whether or not they want to take His advice.

But God wants you to come to Him in faith, with your answer being, "Yes! I'll do it!" even before He tells you what to do! He wants to know that you trust Him, that you believe in your heart that He really does know what's best for you.

What does faith like this look like in real life? If you keep reading in the book of James, you'll find out:

> *"What good is it, my brothers, if a man claims to have faith but has no deeds? Can such faith save him? Suppose a brother or sister is without clothes and daily food. If one of you says to him, 'Go, I wish you well; keep warm and well fed,' but does nothing about his physical needs, what good is it? In the same way, faith by itself, if it is not accompanied by action, is dead"* (James 2:14-17).

The best kind of faith is faith that is put into action, because faith like this demonstrates to God and to those around you that you really do believe what He says is true.

If you're wrestling with a decision in your life, I want to encourage you to ask God for wisdom, whether it's about who to marry, where to live, how to live, how not to live, or any other question that's on your heart. Come to God with an expectant heart. He won't rebuke you for asking for wisdom. Instead, He'll pour out His wisdom on you generously without finding fault.

I'd also encourage you to read through the rest of James chapter 1—and all 5 chapters of the book of James if you can—for his letter contains some of the best wisdom from God on topics like persevering through trials, dealing with temptation, caring for those in need, taming your tongue, praying for healing, and praying in faith.

It might even contain the specific answers to the questions on your heart. If you need wisdom, ask God. And when you ask, ask in faith!

PRAYER

Father, thank You for assuring us that You love to pour out Your wisdom on us when we ask for it in faith. Please answer the prayers on our hearts, and give us the wisdom we need to make the best decisions we can in the situations we face. In Jesus' name, Amen.

MEMORY VERSE

"If any of you lacks wisdom, let him ask God, who gives generously to all without reproach, and it will be given him" (James 1:5, ESV).

WILL GOD REALLY REWARD YOU?

Scripture Reading: Matthew 6

I got a letter in the mail one day from Isaac Asimov, the famous science fiction writer, back when he was still alive. It wasn't a personal letter, but rather a fund raising letter he had written for an atheistic organization. The letter began by saying: "You'll get your reward in heaven!" Asimov then followed up that quote with his own words: "We've all heard *that* empty promise before."

Asimov didn't believe in God, or heaven, or hell. He went on to say in his letter that if you wanted to get anything out of life, you'd better get it here and now for, according to him, there was no hereafter.

But Jesus said something completely different. And although Jesus never wrote a single book, his words have been recorded for us in a book that has sold more copies than any other book in the history of the world. Let's take a look at what Jesus said about God's rewards in Matthew chapter 6:

In talking about giving, Jesus said:

"But when you give to the needy, do not let your left hand know what your right hand is doing, so that your giving may be in secret. And your Father who sees in secret will reward you" (Matthew 6:3-4).

In talking about praying, Jesus said:

"But when you pray, go into your room and shut the door and pray to your Father who is in secret. And your Father who sees in secret will reward you" (Matthew 6:6).

In talking about fasting, Jesus said:

"But when you fast, anoint your head and wash your face, that your fasting may not be seen by others but by your Father who is in secret. And your Father who sees in secret will reward you" (Matthew 6:17-18).

Jesus followed this up by saying that the rewards God has in store for us don't come just

here on earth, but in heaven as well. As Jesus
continues in Matthew 6, He says:

"Do not lay up for yourselves treasures on earth,
where moth and rust destroy and where thieves
break in and steal, but lay up for yourselves treas-
ures in heaven, where neither moth nor rust des-
troys and where thieves do not break in and steal.
For where your treasure is, there your heart will be
also" (Matthew 6:19-21).

I know a pastor who could have made a
tremendous amount of money from the conferences at which he has spoken and the
books that he has written. But instead, he and
his wife have chosen to take only a minimal
salary, living in an extremely humble house,
and declining or giving away the rest of the
millions he could have earned.

His friends have challenged him for the
way he lives, claiming he has a poverty mental-
ity. But he counters their claims by saying that
nothing could be further from the truth. He
wants to get rich more than anyone else he
knows. The difference is that he wants to
store up his riches in heaven, where they will

last forever, rather than cashing in on them here where they will rot or rust.

What about you? What do you believe? Will God really reward you for the things you do for Him, and for others, even those things you do in secret? Jesus says He will, and I for one—along with millions of others—believe Him. I pray that you do, too, for God knows it will affect everything you think and do here on earth, as well as what God does for you in eternity.

You can trust Jesus: God really will reward you when you put Him first in your life. As Jesus said at the end of Matthew 6:

> *"Therefore do not be anxious, saying, 'What shall we eat?' or 'What shall we drink?' or 'What shall we wear?' For the Gentiles seek after all these things, and your heavenly Father knows that you need them all. But seek first the kingdom of God and His righteousness, and all these things will be added to you"* *(Matthew 6:31-33).*

Put your trust in God. He really will reward you!

Prayer

Father, thank You for promising to reward us when we seek first Your kingdom and Your righteousness. Help us to trust You, and not to worry about what we'll eat or drink or wear, but to focus on Your kingdom, storing up our riches in heaven instead. In Jesus' name, Amen.

Memory Verse

"But seek first the kingdom of God and His righteousness, and all these things will be added to you" (Matthew 6:33, ESV).

WHERE SHOULD I START?

Scripture Reading: John 1

If someone had never read the Bible before and they were to ask you where they should start, what would you tell them? For many people, their answer would be to start with the book of John—and for good reason.

John is one of the most beloved books in the Bible. It contains some of the Bible's most famous verses, including John 3:16, and it focuses on God's love for His children perhaps more than any other book. It's short enough that you can read a chapter a day and finish in just 21 days, but it's long enough to give you a good look at the life of Christ— and why you should put your faith in Him. In fact, John says that's why he wrote the book, as he notes at the end of chapter 20:

> *"Now Jesus did many other signs in the presence of the disciples, which are not written in this book; but these are written so that you may believe that Jesus is the Christ, the Son of God, and that by*

believing you may have life in His name" (John 20:30-31).

John saw, with his own eyes, many of the stories that he recorded in his book. While Jesus had many followers, He had twelve who spent three and a half years with Him eating, sleeping, praying, talking, and ministering. And of those twelve, three were especially close to Jesus: Peter, James, and John (see Mark 5:37, Mark 9:2, Mark 13:3, and Mark 14:33). And of those three, John was perhaps the closest, referring to himself in his book as, "the disciple whom Jesus loved" (see John 13:23, 20:2, 21:7, and 21:20).

Perhaps it was because of John's close friendship with Jesus that John talks about the love of God so much, using the word "love" in his gospel more than any of the other gospel writers combined. Here are just a few of those references, all direct quotes that John recorded Jesus as saying:

"For God so loved the world, that He gave His only Son, that whoever believes in Him should not perish but have eternal life" (John 3:16).

"A new commandment I give to you, that you love one another: just as I have loved you, you also are to love one another. By this all people will know that you are my disciples, if you have love for one another" (John 13:34-35)

"If anyone loves Me, he will keep My Word, and My Father will love him, and We will come to him and make Our home with him" (John 14:23).

"As the Father has loved Me, so have I loved you. Abide in My love" (John 15:9).

"Greater love has no one than this, that someone lay down his life for his friends" (John 15:13).

If you need some encouragement that God really loves you, read the book of John. If you need some encouragement that you can trust Christ with everything in your life, read the book of John. If you'd like to read the Bible but don't know where to start, read the book of John. Or if you'd just like a fresh reminder of God's love for you and all the things that are possible when you put your faith in Him, read the book of John.

Start in chapter 1, and you'll find that salvation through Jesus wasn't just an afterthought in the mind of God, but that Jesus was with God in the beginning. John said, referring to Jesus as "the Word":

"In the beginning was the Word, and the Word was with God, and the Word was God. He was in the beginning with God. ... And the Word became flesh and dwelt among us ... " (John 1:1-3, 14a).

You'll also find in chapter 1 that Jesus is "the Lamb of God," who came to take away our sin:

"Behold, the Lamb of God, who takes away the sin of the world!" (John 1:29b).

And lastly in chapter 1, you'll find that Jesus calls you to follow Him, just as He called the first disciples to do, saying:

"Follow Me" (John 1:43b).

Then keep on reading the rest of the book, whether it takes you a few hours, a few days, or 21 days, reading just a chapter a day. Even

if you've read it many times before, I pray that
God will speak new things to you as you do.

PRAYER

*Father, thank You for the words of Your great
love for us that You've recorded for us in the Bible,
and Your desire for us to return that love to You
and to share it with others. Thank You for John's
life and for inspiring him to record these words for
us so we can keep putting our faith in Jesus. It's
in His name we pray, Amen.*

MEMORY VERSE

*"In the beginning was the Word, and the Word
was with God, and the Word was God" (John 1,
ESV).*

THE BEST SERMON EVER

Scripture Reading: Matthew 5

I've just been reading what is perhaps the best sermon ever. It was delivered by Jesus to a crowd of thousands on a hillside near the Sea of Galilee. Because of its location, this sermon is often called "The Sermon on the Mount." It spans three chapters in the book of Matthew, starting in chapter 5.

When you read Jesus' famous sermon, you'll see why it's so popular. It's like reading a *Cliff's Notes* version of the entire Bible. You'll also probably recognize many of the famous quotes that come from this passage. Here are just a few from chapter 5:

"Blessed are the poor in spirit, for theirs is the kingdom of heaven. Blessed are those who mourn, for they shall be comforted. Blessed are the meek, for they shall inherit the earth" (Matthew 5:3-5).

"You are the light of the world. A city set on a hill cannot be hidden. Nor do people light a lamp and put it under a basket, but on a stand, and it

gives light to all in the house. In the same way, let your light shine before others, so that they may see your good works and give glory to your Father who is in heaven" (Matthew 5:14-16).

"You have heard that it was said, 'You shall not commit adultery.' But I say to you that everyone who looks at a woman with lustful intent has already committed adultery with her in his heart" (Matthew 5:27-28).

"You have heard that it was said, 'An eye for an eye and a tooth for a tooth.' But I say to you, Do not resist the one who is evil. But if anyone slaps you on the right cheek, turn to him the other also" (Matthew 5:38-39).

"You have heard that it was said, 'You shall love your neighbor and hate your enemy.' But I say to you, Love your enemies and pray for those who persecute you ... " (Matthew 5:43-44).

Reading through the Sermon on the Mount is like reading through the best-of-the-best quotes from *Bartlett's Familiar Quotations.* It even includes the Golden Rule and the Lord's Prayer!

But I'd also like to point out that even the best sermons in the world are only fruitful if those who hear the words put them into practice. As Jesus said at the end of His sermon:

"Everyone then who hears these words of mine and does them will be like a wise man who built his house on the rock. And the rain fell, and the floods came, and the winds blew and beat on that house, but it did not fall, because it had been founded on the rock. And everyone who hears these words of mine and does not do them will be like a foolish man who built his house on the sand. And the rain fell, and the floods came, and the winds blew and beat against that house, and it fell, and great was the fall of it" (Matthew 7:24-27).

I wrote a book a few years ago called *What God Says About Sex*. My purpose was to share what I had learned about this precious gift from God and to spare others from the heartache that often comes from misusing this gift. Many people have read the book over the years, and I've been amazed at the results —some good, and some not so good.

Some people have read it eagerly, taking the words to heart, putting them into practice, and being blessed beyond measure. Others have picked it up with interest at first, only to set it down later and ignore what they read, ending up with unplanned pregnancies, untreatable diseases, and unnecessary pain. Then there are those who have gotten a copy of the book but didn't crack it open—until it was too late.

I know of one man who had it sitting on his bedroom dresser—unopened and unread —when he got his girlfriend pregnant. They broke up soon afterwards, but when their precious baby was born, they entered into a lengthy and heart-wrenching custody battle.

The man later said that he wished he had read my book *before* this all happened.

When I hear stories like these, I get a small glimpse into what God must feel when people read—or don't read—His Book, and the various results that come when they put His Words into practice—or don't.

I'd like to encourage you to take some time this week to read the "Sermon on the Mount" and see for yourself why it is perhaps "The Best Sermon Ever." You'll find it in Matthew chapters 5, 6, and 7. It only takes about 20-30 minutes to read, but if you put what you read into practice, you'll be blessed for a lifetime!

My hope and my prayer is that you will take time to read these chapters and that you'll be a light shining for Christ—and, as Jesus said, when others see your good works, they'll "give glory to your Father who is in heaven."

PRAYER

Father, thank You for giving us Your wisdom in the words of the Bible. Help us to read Your word daily, take it to heart, and put it into practice in our lives. In Jesus' name, Amen.

MEMORY VERSE

"You are the light of the world. A city set on a hill cannot be hidden. Nor do people light a lamp and put it under a basket, but on a stand, and it gives light to all in the house. In the same way, let your light shine before others, so that they may see your good works and give glory to your Father who is in heaven" (Matthew 5:14-16, ESV).

GOD'S PROTECTION

Scripture Reading: Psalm 91

There's a difference between "believing in God" and "believing God." You can believe in God yet still keep Him at a distance. But when you believe God—when you take Him at His Word and put what He says into practice in your life—you enter into a relationship with Him, a relationship that is up close and personal; a relationship where every step you take is wise and purposeful because you're keeping in step with Him.

Psalm 91 describes one of the great benefits of this kind of close relationship with God: you enter into His divine protection. Here are some of the things God will do for you when you dwell "in the shelter of the Most High":

> *"He who dwells in the shelter of the Most High will abide in the shadow of the Almighty.*
> *I will say to the LORD, 'My refuge and my fortress,*

my God, in whom I trust.'
For He will deliver you from the snare of the
fowler
   and from the deadly pestilence.
He will cover you with His pinions,
   and under His wings you will find refuge;
   His faithfulness is a shield and buckler.
You will not fear the terror of the night,
   nor the arrow that flies by day,
   nor the pestilence that stalks in darkness,
   nor the destruction that wastes at noonday.
A thousand may fall at your side,
   ten thousand at your right hand,
   but it will not come near you"
   (Psalm 91:1-7).

Moses, who many Jewish scholars believe authored this Psalm, saw his share of trouble. He saw plagues of locusts and plagues of death, threats of famine and threats on his life. But Moses also saw God's divine hand of deliverance.

When the angel of death passed through the streets of Egypt, thousands fell, but Moses and his people were saved. Not only did they believe *in* God but they also *believed* God. They did what He told them to do, putting the blood of a lamb on the doorframes of their homes so the angel of death would "pass over" and spare the lives of those inside (see Exodus 12).

Jesus is *our* passover lamb, and when you put your faith in Him—staying close to Him and holding on tight—then He's able to take you under His protective wings. It's hard for God to protect you, though, if you keep running back and forth to Him, coming to Him only *after* disaster strikes. He wants you to be in a close relationship with Him at all times, dwelling with Him, living with Him, taking up residence in His protective refuge. When you do, listen to a few more of the ways you'll be blessed:

> *"Because you have made the LORD your dwelling place—*
>   *the Most High, who is my refuge—*
>   *no evil shall be allowed to befall you,*
>   *no plague come near your tent.*
> *For He will command His angels concerning you*
>   *to guard you in all your ways.*
> *On their hands they will bear you up,*
>   *lest you strike your foot against a stone.*
> *You will tread on the lion and the adder;*

the young lion and the serpent you will trample underfoot.
Because he holds fast to Me in love, I will deliver him;
I will protect him, because he knows My Name.
When he calls to Me, I will answer him;
I will be with him in trouble;
I will rescue him and honor him.
With long life I will satisfy him
and show him My salvation"
(Psalm 91:9-10, 14-16).

It's good to believe in God, but it's even better to believe God, drawing near to Him and dwelling in His shelter. How do you do that? By calling out to Him when you wake up each morning. By reading His Word and listening to His Spirit so you can hear back from Him. By holding on tight to Him throughout the day and taking care to do what He says, stepping where He says to step (and not stepping where He says *not* to step!). And when the day is done, being sure to say good-night again, entrusting Him to hold you tight throughout the night.

God loves you and wants to protect you,

shield you, and deliver you. Just be sure to stay under His protective wings.

PRAYER

Father, thank You for loving us and offering us Your strong hand of protection. Help us to come closer and closer to You so that we can see what Moses saw, and experience Your deliverance first-hand. In Jesus' name, Amen.

MEMORY VERSE

"Because he holds fast to Me in love, I will deliver him; I will protect him, because he knows My Name" (Psalm 91:14, ESV).

Number 4

God Works For Your Good

Scripture Reading: Romans 8

God is for you. He loves you. And He can work all things together for good, when you love Him and are called according to His purpose. These concepts are found throughout the Bible. But they're also stated clearly and succinctly in Romans chapter 8.

Although the Apostle Paul wrote this letter to the believers living in Rome, Italy, about the year 54 A.D., Paul's words apply just as much to you today, wherever you happen to live in the world, if you, too, are a believer in Christ. Here are a few of the things Paul said.

He wants you to be free from the guilt and shame that you might feel because of your sins:

> *"There is therefore now no condemnation for those who are in Christ Jesus" (Romans 8:1).*

He wants you to know that you aren't alone in your struggle against sin, for the life-giving power of the Holy Spirit lives within you:

"If the Spirit of Him who raised Jesus from the dead dwells in you, He who raised Christ Jesus from the dead will also give life to your mortal bodies through His Spirit who dwells in you" (Romans 8:11).

He wants you to know that if you are experiencing any suffering in this world, that it will hardly compare to the glory you will see one day:

"For I consider that the sufferings of this present time are not worth comparing with the glory that is to be revealed to us" (Romans 8:18).

Or as Samuel Rutherford, a Scottish writer in the 1600's, paraphrased it: "Our little time of suffering is not worthy of our first night's welcome home to Heaven."

Paul wants you to know that even when you are at a loss as to how to pray for yourself, the Holy Spirit will pray for you:

"Likewise the Spirit helps us in our weakness. For we do not know what to pray for as we ought, but the Spirit Himself intercedes for us with groanings too deep for words" (Romans 8:26).

And in one of the most famous verses in the Bible, Paul wants you to know that God will work all things for good for those who love Him and are called according to His purpose:

"And we know that for those who love God all things work together for good, for those who are called according to His purpose" (Romans 8:28).

I often quote this verse—both to myself and to others—because it's a great reminder that God can bring good out of any difficulty that we face.

There's a concept in karate called "borrowed force" that's useful when someone throws a punch at you. Instead of taking the hit and letting the punch knock you out, you can take hold of the punch with your hands, add your own strength to it, and throw your opponent to the ground behind you. Instead of letting the punch defeat you, you can use it for good.

When life—or people, or your job, or the economy—throws a punch at you that could possibly knock you out, God wants you to put your faith in Him. When you do, He'll help you take hold of that punch, and instead of letting it defeat you, He can use it for good.

If you remember the story of Joseph and his brothers, you'll see how Joseph was able to see God's hand at work, even after his brothers sold him as a slave into Egypt. God one day raised Joseph up to be second in command in Egypt, giving him wisdom to store up food during years of plenty for an upcoming famine, resulting in saving many people in Egypt as well as his own brothers. Joseph said:

"As for you, you meant evil against me, but God meant it for good, to bring it about that many people should be kept alive, as they are today" (Genesis 50:20).

God is for you, too. He loves you. And if you'll trust in Him with everything that you're going through today, He really can and will work all things together for good.

I hope you'll read the rest of Romans 8 today—especially the last section in verses 31-39. They're some of the most uplifting words in the whole Bible. If God is for you, who can be against you!

PRAYER

Father, thank You for loving us so fully, and for promising us that You will indeed work all things for good in our lives when we love you and are called according to Your purpose. Help us to trust You and Your promises completely, as we face the challenges in our lives today. In Jesus' name, Amen.

MEMORY VERSE

"And we know that for those who love God all things work together for good, for those who are called according to His purpose" (Romans 8:28, ESV).

FROM COVER TO COVER

Scripture Reading: Genesis 1

A young preacher once invited an older preacher to his church to share a sermon with his congregation. The sermon was powerful and many people were touched deeply by the message. Afterwards, the younger preacher asked the older preacher the secret of his success.

The older preacher asked him, "How many times have you read the Bible, from cover to cover?"

The younger preacher said, "I've read a lot of it, but I've never read the whole thing all the way through even once yet."

The older preacher then pointed at his Bible and said: "When you've read this book twenty times, from cover to cover, then you'll be able to preach like that."

I know this is a true story, because the man who told it to me *was* that younger preacher, many years ago, and he went home and did exactly what the older preacher suggested. By the time I heard him tell the story, he was quite old. Although he didn't tell me how many times he'd read the Bible from cover to cover since he first got that advice, if I were to judge from the message I heard him preach that day, I would say he well exceeded the suggested twenty! He was a powerful preacher!

What's good for powerful preaching is also good for powerful living.

The most pivotal time in my life came when I started reading the Bible from cover to cover for myself. I had been in a Bible study for a few months with a small group of men from our church, and decided to go out and buy a good study Bible—with lots of footnotes included in it so I could understand better what I was reading.

I started at Genesis, Chapter 1. As I began to read, I tried to immerse myself in the story, reading it not just as ancient history, but more like a newspaper, describing the events of the day as if they were actually taking place while I was reading them. I found that when I read the Bible this way, the stories came alive, starting with the story of the creation of the world:

"In the beginning, God created the heavens and the earth" (Genesis 1:1).

As I read that passage, I began to picture what it must have been like for God to create something out of nothing.

When God said, "Let there be light," and there was light, I tried to picture what it would have been like to be in total darkness, and then watch as God's light burst onto the scene. As I continued reading, I could see water flowing, waves crashing, plants growing, fish swimming, birds flying, animals moving, and then—as the climactic event—God creating the first two human beings in His own image. I felt like Thomas Merton must have felt when he wrote:

"By reading the scriptures I am so renewed that all nature seems renewed around me and with me. The sky seems to be a pure, a cooler blue, the trees a deeper green. The whole world is charged with the glory of God and I feel fire and music under my feet."

After a few weeks of reading the Bible like this, I sensed God's love for me in a new and deeper way. I also began to see my need for a Savior. I put my faith in Christ shortly thereafter and I've never looked back. I honestly don't know how many times I've read the Bible since then, either. But I do know that as I've read and reread this precious book over the years, it has changed me, challenged me, comforted me, and most of all increased my faith in Him who spoke its words into existence. As D.L. Moody said: ·

> *"I prayed for faith and thought it would strike me like lightening. But faith did not come. One day I read, 'Now faith comes by hearing, and hearing by the Word of God.' I had closed my Bible and prayed for faith. I now began to study my Bible and faith has been growing ever since."*

If you'd like to increase your faith, I'd encourage you to read the Bible, from cover to cover, starting in Genesis chapter 1. Make it a goal for yourself—not just to get through the whole Bible—but to let the whole Bible get through you. You'll be glad you did.

PRAYER

Father, thank You for giving us Your words in the pages of the Bible. Help us to read them and apply them to our lives daily so that we can grow closer and closer to You, and in the process, grow to look more and more like Your Son, Jesus Christ. It's in His name we pray, Amen.

MEMORY VERSE

"In the beginning, God created the heavens and the earth" (Genesis 1:1, ESV).

Savoring Every Word

Scripture Reading: Psalm 23

Last time I talked about the value of reading the entire Bible from cover to cover. This time I'd like to focus on another approach to reading the Bible: savoring every word. For the goal of reading the Bible is not just to get all the way through it, but to let it get all through you!

One way to do that is to go slowly and meditate on the words you're reading—to think deeply about them and the implications they may have on your life.

For instance, let's take a close look at just a few verses from Psalm 23, the second most popular passage in the Bible. Because Psalm 23 is such a popular passage, you might be tempted to read it so quickly that you miss the flavor and nutrients offered by each of its words. But by slowing down and meditating on every word, you can better digest what you're reading.

Here's what happened to me as I spent

time meditating on the first few verses of Psalm 23 this week, which starts like this:

"The LORD is my shepherd; I shall not want. He makes me lie down in green pastures. He leads me beside still waters. He restores my soul." (Psalm 23:1-2a).

As I started with the words, "The Lord is my shepherd," I thought about how God isn't just "a" god or "one god out of many," but that He is "THE God, THE Lord, THE One and Only Creator of the universe, THE Author and Sustainer of my life, with all of my life's intricate complexities.

As I thought about the little word "is" in "The Lord is my shepherd," I thought about the fact that the Lord IS my shepherd—not that He *was* my shepherd, or that He *will* be my shepherd, but that He IS my shepherd, taking care of me, protecting me, and nourishing me, right here and right now.

As I looked at the word "my," in "The Lord is my shepherd," I realized that the Lord is not just our shepherd, or the shepherd of the whole world, but that He's also MY shepherd. He knows me by name (see John 10:3

and 11), and if I ever strayed away, I know He would leave the rest of the flock behind in safety in order to find me and rescue me from danger (see Matthew 18, 12-14).

With the Lord as my shepherd, it's no wonder the verse continues with the words: "I shall not want."

But it was when I read, "He makes me lie down in green pastures," that God began to speak personally and specifically to me about a situation in my life that happened about a year ago, when we were considering launching out into a whole new aspect of our ministry. At the last minute, God redirected our steps and moved us out to where we're living now at Clover Ranch. As I read about the green pastures this week, I was watching my son mow the green grass in our front yard for the first time this year.

Although a year ago it seemed like God was pulling the rug out from under our feet in some ways, the truth was that He was "making us lie down in green pastures." He was leading us beside His still waters. He was restoring our souls. I was reminded of the quote from Daniel Defoe, the author of Robinson Crusoe, who said,

"God will often deliver us in a manner that seems initially to destroy us."

Oh, how thankful I was—and am—to have the Lord as my shepherd!

I didn't make it through the rest of Psalm 23 that day, but what a sweet time I had with God by just meditating on a few of His words.

As much as I love encouraging people to read through their whole Bibles many times, I love it, too, when they can savor every word. I'd encourage you to read through the rest of Psalm 23 for yourself today, stopping and meditating on those words or phrases that seem to stand out to you. Let them sink deep into your heart and mind, and let God restore *your* soul.

PRAYER

Father, thank You for the richness of Your Word, and for using it to speak into our hearts and lives. Help us to read it thoroughly, to think about it deeply, and to let it impact the way we live our lives here on earth. In Jesus' name, Amen.

MEMORY VERSE

"The LORD is my shepherd; I shall not want"
(Psalm 23:1, ESV).

THE LOVE TEST

Scripture Reading: 1 Corinthians 13

There's a philosophy in ethics called "enlightened self-interest." It's the intriguing idea that many of the "good deeds" we do are not motivated entirely for the benefit of others, but somehow serve our own self-interests as well.

Giving to charity, for instance, is a noble endeavor. But if our giving is solely dependent on whether or not we get a tax-deduction for our gift, then our giving really falls in the category of enlightened self-interest. We're glad to give—as long as our giving benefits us back in some way.

Not that there's anything wrong with enlightened self-interest in and of itself, as the idea of giving, and getting something in return, is the basis of economies all over the world. It only becomes a problem when we mistake enlightened self-interest for selfless love, thinking that what we're doing is truly loving, when in reality it could be simply selfishness masquerading as love.

Today we're looking at a passage in the Bible that deals almost entirely with love. Pure love. A love that is selfless and unadulterated. A love that gives without expecting anything in return. It's found in chapter 13 of the Apostle Paul's first letter to the believers who were living in the city of Corinth. Paul wrote the letter as a reminder to the Corinthians that no matter how important all of their gifts and abilities might be, they were meaningless without love. Paul wrote:

"If I speak in the tongues of men and of angels, but have not love, I am a noisy gong or a clanging cymbal. And if I have prophetic powers, and understand all mysteries and all knowledge, and if I have all faith, so as to remove mountains, but have not love, I am nothing. If I give away all I have, and if I deliver up my body to be burned, but have not love, I gain nothing" (1 Corinthians 13:1-3).

Paul knew that God wants love to be at the core of everything we do. In the end, as Oliver Thomas said, "Authentic religion is not a theology test. It's a love test." As important as theology is—and moving mountains and giving sacrificially and every other good thing in which we engage—love must pervade them all, or else we've failed the test.

Paul continued his letter by writing one of the most beautiful definitions of love found in all of literature. Because of this, 1 Corinthians 13 is frequently read at wedding ceremonies throughout the world. Paul says:

"Love is patient and kind; love does not envy or boast; it is not arrogant or rude. It does not insist on its own way; it is not irritable or resentful; it does not rejoice at wrongdoing, but rejoices with the truth. Love bears all things, believes all things, hopes all things, endures all things. Love never ends" (1 Corinthians 13:4-8a).

Paul's words serve as a checklist of sorts to help us determine how truly loving we are towards those around us. While many times we might think we're acting in love, if we compare our love to the love described in this passage, we'll get to the heart of what truly motivates us. Is it pure love? Or just some form of "enlightened self-interest," giving to others with the hope that we might get some kind of benefit in return?

There are times when we buy cards or gifts,

or do favors for people, which seem selfless on the surface. But when we don't get the desired response in return for our efforts, our selfishness is exposed. Perhaps we weren't being truly as loving or generous as we thought. When thinking about some of the relationships in your own life, you can ask yourself these questions, based on 1 Corinthians 13:

Is my love for this person patient and kind?
Is it envious or boastful?
Is it arrogant or rude?
Does it insist on its own way?
Is it irritable or resentful?
Does it rejoice at wrongdoing? Or does it rejoice with the truth?
Does it bear all things, believe all things, hope all things, endure all things?
Does my love for them never end?

If you're like me, just reading through this list can be convicting. But Paul didn't write these words to dash us to pieces. He wrote them to lift us up, to encourage us to do what's right, and to begin loving others for all the right reasons again.

Let love motivate everything you do—not

selfishness, and not selfishness masquerading as love. As you put these words into practice, you'll see why Paul closes this famous chapter on love by saying, that of all the incredible gifts that God has given you,

> " ... *the greatest of these is love.*"
> *(1 Corinthians 13:13b)*

LET'S PRAY...

> *Father, thank You for loving us with a selfless love. We pray that You would help us show that same kind of love to those around us. Help us to be patient and kind, not envious or boastful. Keep us from arrogance or rudeness, or insisting on our own way, or being irritable or resentful. Help us to never rejoice at wrongdoing, but to always rejoice with the truth. Thank You for Your never ending love for us, and help us to love others in the exact same way. In Jesus' name, Amen.*

MEMORY VERSE

> *"Love is patient and kind; love does not envy or boast; it is not arrogant or rude. It does not insist on its own way; it is not irritable or resentful; it*

does not rejoice at wrongdoing, but rejoices with the truth. Love bears all things, believes all things, hopes all things, endures all things. Love never ends" (1 Corinthians 13:4-7, ESV).

Conclusion

THE ULTIMATE LOVE AFFAIR

Scripture Reading: John 5:39-40

Some people wonder why Christians have such a love affair with the Bible. The truth is that we're not just in love with the words on the pages. We're in love with the One who is portrayed by those words.

It's like carrying around a picture of your beloved in your purse or wallet. When you take out that picture, looking fondly at the image, and maybe even brushing the picture up against your cheek, or giving it a kiss with your lips, it's not that you're in love with the picture on the paper. You're in love with the one whose image is displayed on the paper.

In the same way, those who love their Bibles aren't just in love with the Bible. They're in love with the One who is displayed on its pages.

Yet as wonderful as this kind of love affair with the Bible can be, there's a surprising danger in it. There are times when you might fall so much in love with the words on the pages that you miss having a relationship with the Word Himself, Jesus Christ, who is described on those pages. Even Jesus warned of this danger when He said to some of the religious leaders of His day:

"You search the Scriptures because you think that in them you have eternal life; and it is they that bear witness about Me, yet you refuse to come to Me that you may have life" (John 5:39-40).

The Message translation of the Bible paraphrases these same words of Jesus like this:

"You have your heads in your Bibles constantly because you think you'll find eternal life there... These Scriptures are all about me! And here I am, standing right before you" (John 5:39-40, MSG).

Imagine holding a picture of your beloved in your hands, treasuring it, pulling it close to your heart, and even gazing at it longingly, all the while not even realizing or acknowledging that your beloved is standing right there next to you the whole time!

As much as I love the Bible—and it *is* my favorite book in the world—I have to remind myself from time to time that the Trinity is not made up of "the Father, the Son, and the Holy Scripture." But rather, the Trinity is made up of "the Father, the Son, and the Holy Spirit," three aspects of the same singular God who loves you and wants to be involved actively in your life today!

Keep reading your Bible, but don't forget: Jesus is STILL alive! When His Holy Spirit prompts you to give, then give! When you ask Him a question in prayer, then wait and listen for His answer! When you're feeling stressed and start meditating on God's Word, remember that God's Word—Jesus Christ—is standing right there with you, too!

The words of the Bible are like love letters to you from your beloved, scented with the perfume of heaven, and sealed with a kiss from the Creator of the universe. He loves you more than you could know, and He demonstrated that love by sending His Son Jesus to live and die and rise again from the dead, so you can live and die and rise again from the dead with Him one day, too. If you're going to have a love affair, make sure you have it not just with the words on the pages of the Bible, but have it with the One

who is described by those words: Jesus
Christ!

PRAYER

*Father thank You for showing us who you are on
the pages of the Bible. Help us to read Your
Word as love letters from You, and help us to remind ourselves that our relationship is with You—
a real and living Person. We invite you to speak
into our lives again today, and continue to speak to
us throughout our lives and on into heaven, when
we will be with You forever. In Jesus' name,
Amen.*

MEMORY VERSE

*"You search the Scriptures because you think that
in them you have eternal life; and it is they that
bear witness about Me, yet you refuse to come to
Me that you may have life" (John 5:39-40).*

Small Group Study Guide

I'm excited to offer this study guide for groups who want to study this material together! While studying God's Word on your own can be extremely rewarding, studying it with others can be even more so. I've learned from my own experience that the words of Solomon are true: "As iron sharpens iron, so one man sharpens another" (Proverbs 27:17).

This study is divided into twenty lessons (not counting the Introduction and Conclusion), and the questions that follow can be used for personal reflection, group discussion, or a combination of both.

If your group wants to read and discuss each lesson together, they could meet once a week and complete this study in twenty weeks. If your group wants to cover the material more quickly, group members could study several lessons on their own during the week, then discuss those lessons together with the group (covering, for example, five lessons per week for a period of four weeks).

However you choose to do it, I pray that God will speak to you through it!

INTRODUCTION – THE TOP 20 PASSAGES IN THE BIBLE

The Bible is filled with passages that God can use to speak to you at any time, whether those passages are well-known or not. But because the Bible is both "God-breathed," and "living and active," God can bring any passage to life right before your eyes, speaking directly to your heart and mind.

1. Has the Bible ever spoken to you in a way that you felt that God Himself was speaking to you through the words on the pages? What is one of your favorite Bible passages, and why?

2. What do you think makes the Bible the best-selling book of all time? Even if the words on its pages weren't attributed to God Himself, why might the Bible still be a best-seller?

NUMBER 20 – THE CHRISTMAS STORY

Luke's version of the birth of Christ contains many miracles—with angels everywhere, a tongue that is tied and then loosened again, and even a virgin birth. Yet Luke's account is one of the most detailed and well-researched of the four gospels, having been written by a medical doctor who personally travelled with the Apostle Paul on his missionary journeys.

1. *When you think of the Christmas story, what are some incidents that stand out in your mind as miraculous? When you read Luke's account of the events surrounding the birth of Christ, what details does he include that he might have gathered from eye-witnesses?*

2. *Why might the angel Gabriel speak with such authority regarding the faithfulness of God in keeping His promises? When Gabriel said to Elizabeth "For nothing is impossible with God," what was he referring to specifically in her case? How might that encourage you that there really is nothing else that is impossible with God either?*

NUMBER 19 – MAKING THE BEST USE OF THE TIME

Paul told the Ephesians to make the best use of their time, living as wise, not unwise people. He spoke of specific things they should avoid doing, and specific things that they should begin doing, if they weren't already.

1. *What are a few of the things Paul specifically urged the Ephesians not to do? What are a few of the things he specifically urged them to do?*

2. *What caused the change in Alfred Nobel's life, even though he was near the end of it? How can thinking through how you'll be remembered in the future change the way you live your life now? Are there specific changes you could make right now to keep from wasting time—and making the most of the time you still have left?*

Number 18 – God's Love For You

In Paul's letter to the Ephesians, he said that he got down on his knees to pray for them, that they would be able to know the breadth and length and height and depth of God's love for them. He knew how hard grasping God's love and grace could be, yet he spends a great deal of time trying to help them grasp this life-giving truth.

1. *What are some things that happen to people that can make them question God's love for them?*

What are some things that have happened to you that have made you question His love?

2. *Other than prayer, how can you get a better picture of what God's love for you looks like? And through prayer, what specifically might you pray so that you could better grasp God's love?*

Number 17 – The Gospel In A Nutshell

The most famous quote in the Bible took place in a conversation that Jesus had with Nicodemus, a member of the Jewish ruling council who came to Jesus at night. Jesus told him that for someone to enter the kingdom of God, they must be born again—that whoever believes in Him would not perish but have eternal life.

1. *What other story did Jesus bring up in his conversation with Nicodemus to talk about God's willingness to forgive and heal His people when they sinned? How does this story relate to what Jesus was about to do on the cross?*

2. *Why did Jesus describe entering the kingdom of God as being "born again"? Do you feel like*

you've been "born again"? And if not, do you want to be?

NUMBER 16 – THE POWER OF GOD FOR SALVATION

The Apostle Paul said that he was not ashamed of the gospel of Jesus Christ, for it was the power of God for salvation to everyone who believes. In describing this gospel, Paul first explains the "bad news" regarding our sinfulness, then leads into the "good news" regarding our future if we're willing to put our faith in Christ.

1. *Why is it helpful to understand the "bad news" of the gospel in order to understand why it is such "good news"? What does the "wrath of God" look like, according to this passage?*

2. *What are ways that people turn against God's plans for their lives, according to Romans 1? In what ways might God's wrath manifest itself in the lives of people who do these things, without God even having to intervene?*

3. *In Romans 1:32, Paul says "they not only do them but give approval to those who practice*

them." Why might giving approval to some of these things add to the damage that is already being done? And what can someone do to be delivered from God's wrath?

Number 15 – Walk In A Manner Worthy Of Your Calling

Even though Paul was imprisoned for his faith, he was able to treat those around him with the love that God had shown to him. He encouraged the Ephesians to renew their minds so they could walk in a manner worthy of the calling they had receive from God.

1. *How does Dennis the Menace's comment to his friend about Mrs. Wilson's goodness to them relate to God's goodness to us? How is Paul able to draw on this truth to extend love to those who mistreated him?*

2. *What does Paul tell us to "put off" in this passage, and why? And what does he tell us to "put on" instead, and why? How does he suggest we do that, particularly in regards to our minds?*

NUMBER 14 – GOD KNOWS YOU

King David wrote many beautiful songs, called Psalms, that are recorded for us in the Bible. One of the most beloved among them is Psalm 139, which describes in detail just how intimately God knows each one of us, reminding us that there is no place in the world that we can go where He is not there with us.

1. *What are some of the details that God knows about you, as mentioned in Psalm 139? Do any surprise you, or give you special comfort?*

2. *What things come to mind that make you think you were "fearfully and wonderfully made"? Do you think God has a plan for your life, based on the words in this Psalm?*

NUMBER 13 – LIKE A TREE PLANTED BY WATER

Sometimes we want to go and do something for God, but He wants us to be like a tree planted by the water, drawing life from His Word. In this way, we can refresh ourselves, provide shade and rest for those who are drawn to us, and like a strong and healthy tree, yield fruit at the proper time.

1. *What are some of the things this Psalm says that we should do—and not do—in order to grow and prosper in our lives? How can we do those things in a practical way?*

2. *What are some of the benefits of doing—and not doing—these things in our lives? How did Thomas Merton describe the renewal he experienced when reading God's Word?*

Number 12 – Don't Be Anxious

Writing from a prison cell, the Apostle Paul encouraged the believers in the city of Philippi not to be anxious about anything, but to give thanks to God, making their requests known to God. He reminded them that the Lord was "at hand," and urged them to dwell as much as possible on things that were good and godly.

1. *What did Paul mean when he said the Lord is "at hand"? What difference can that knowledge make in your thoughts and attitudes towards what you're facing?*

2. *What are some of your favorite things, things that are true, honorable, just, pure, lovely, commendable, excellent, and worthy of praise? How might dwelling on such thoughts keep your thoughts in perspective?*

NUMBER 11 – A LIVING SACRIFICE

In Romans 12, Paul talks about being "a living sacrifice," using your gifts to make an offering to God, at the same time blessing you and those around you. Paul lists many of these gifts, saying that each of us has been given different gifts by God and are to use them according to the grace God has given to us.

1. *How can identifying some of your passions in life help you to also identify the gifts God may have given you? Based on the meaning of the word enthusiasm, how can our enthusiasm relate to our giftedness?*

2. *What are some of the spiritual gifts, as listed in Romans 12, that you feel most passionate about? If you could be the best at one particular skill, what would it be, and why? How might your answers to these two questions be related.*

NUMBER 10 – THE REALITY OF HEAVEN

After telling the disciples He was going away, Jesus assured them that He would not leave them alone, sending the Holy Spirit to be with them while He was gone. He also assured them that He was going to prepare a place for them and would return for them.

1. *Why did Jesus say to the disciples, "Let not your hearts be troubled"? What assurances did He give them so they wouldn't have to worry about His going away, or their future?*

2. *What did Jesus say they could do if they ever needed anything? And what did He ask them to do if He ever needed them to do something?*

3. *When Jesus said He was the way, the truth and the life, why did He add that no one could come to the Father except through Him? Are you sure you're going to heaven, and if not, are you ready yet to put your faith in Christ to get that assurance?*

NUMBER 9 – NEED WISDOM? ASK GOD!

God loves to pour out His wisdom to those who ask Him for it, for He has a vested interest in the decisions we make. But James reminds us that when we ask for wisdom, we are to ask for it in faith, believing that God will answer us, and that He has our best interests at heart.

1. *Why does James say we must ask for wisdom "in faith"? What does he say will happen to the person who doesn't believe what God tells them in response to their prayers?*

2. *How hard is it for you to say, "Yes, Lord!" to God even before He's given you His answer? How would it change your prayers if you were to tell God you would do whatever He said, even before you knew His answer?*

NUMBER 8 – WILL GOD REALLY REWARD YOU?

Some people believe that the only rewards you'll get in life are the ones you get here and now here on earth. But Jesus says that there are all kinds of rewards awaiting us in heaven when we put our faith in Him, trusting Him to reward us for acts done in secret with rewards that won't rust or rot away but will last forever.

1. *How does Jesus say we can store up rewards for ourselves in heaven? Why does He say we should work towards those rewards instead of just rewards that we can get here on earth?*

2. *What specific things might you change in your life if you were to really focus on storing up rewards for yourself in heaven? How might focusing on heaven—seeking God's Kingdom and His righteousness first and foremost—help you not to worry about things you need here on earth?*

NUMBER 7 – WHERE SHOULD I START?

Many people recommend to those who are new at reading the Bible to start in the book of John, for John gives a great overview of the life of Jesus, and focuses on Jesus' great love for each one of us. John's purpose of writing the book is recorded in chapter 20, saying that his hope is that those reading his words will put their faith in Jesus.

1. *In the opening words of John chapter 1, why does John describe Jesus as "the Word"? What does he mean when he says "the Word became flesh and dwelt among us"?*

2. *If you look through the book of John, what are a few of the many verses that talk about God's love for us? Are some of these particularly meaningful to you at this time in your life?*

3. *If you've never read through the book of John, would you be interested in reading it now, reading, for instance, a chapter a day for the next 21 days?*

NUMBER 6 – THE BEST SERMON EVER

Jesus preached His famous "Sermon on the Mount" on a hillside near the Sea of Galilee. In the sermon, Jesus addressed dozens of practical issues that people face in their lives, and ends with an encouragement to be like a person who built their house on solid rock, by putting the words He had spoken into practice.

1. *As you look through the "Sermon on the Mount," what are some of the phrases that strike you as particularly famous? What are some of the phrases that stand out as important to what you're dealing with today?*

2. *What does Jesus say a person will be like if they hear His words and put them into practice? And*

what will a person be like who hears His words and doesn't put them into practice? How can you put Jesus' words into practice in your life this week?

NUMBER 5 – GOD'S PROTECTION

In Psalm 92, Moses says that God's protective hand will shelter those who put their faith in Him. Moses knew this truth firsthand, having believed God when God called him to deliver the Israelites from the oppression of the Egyptians, following God's commands and staying safe and secure under His protective wings.

1. *What are some of the benefits of staying close to God, as described in Psalm 91? Which of these benefits are particularly appealing to you in your life right now?*

2. *What's the difference, in your own words, between just believing in God and believing God? What could you do this week to demonstrate that you do both? And what benefits could there be if you do?*

NUMBER 4 – GOD WORKS FOR YOUR GOOD

In Romans chapter 8, Paul reminds us that God works all things for good, for those who love Him and are called according to His purpose. He also reminds us that the Spirit of Him who raised Jesus from the dead is living inside us, and can give life to our mortal bodies as well.

1. *How can the karate concept of "borrowed force" be applied to our lives today, in light of what Paul says in Romans 8:28? Have you ever seen God work things out for good which looked, at first, to be disastrous?*

2. *Why does Paul say there is no condemnation for those who are in Christ Jesus? What are some of the things Paul lists at the end of Romans 8 that can't separate us from the love of God?*

NUMBER 3 – FROM COVER TO COVER

The Bible begins with Genesis chapter 1, which describes the creation of the world, and it's a great place to start reading the Bible, and keep reading all the way through it all the way to the end. Reading it like this from cover to cover, over and over again, is one of the best ways to grow in your faith, and in your ability to share that faith with others.

1. What benefits might there be from reading the Bible all the way through, from cover to cover? What benefits might there be from reading it from cover to cover, several times, especially at different stages of your life?

2. Have you ever read through the entire Bible, from cover to cover? If not, would you consider doing it? If so, are you ready to do it again?

NUMBER 2 – SAVORING EVERY WORD

Psalm 23 is the second most popular passage in the Bible, describing God as a shepherd who leads us beside His still waters. Each word of this Psalm is precious, just as each word in the Bible is precious, and there are times when God wants us to savor every word.

1. What are some of the benefits of having the Lord as your shepherd, as described in Psalm 23? Have you ever felt like God was leading you to a place of rest, and what purpose did He seem to have for doing this?

2. *What are some of the benefits of reading big chunks of the Bible at one time? And what are some of the benefits of taking your time and savoring just a few words or phrases at a time?*

NUMBER 1 – THE LOVE TEST

Paul's famous passage on love is a reminder that God wants love to pervade everything you do, for without it, even if you had faith to move mountains or to give away everything you owned to the poor, you would gain nothing. In the end, life is not about all that you do, but doing all that you do *in love*.

1. *How do Paul's words about love, and the motivations behind what we do, put our good deeds into perspective? Can a person do good deeds without love? Can a person love without good deeds?*

2. *How can Paul's words about love—pure love—be be used as a checklist to see how well we're doing in our own relationships? What does Paul mean when he says at the end of this passage, "So now*

faith, hope, and love abide, these three; but the greatest of these is love"?

CONCLUSION – THE ULTIMATE LOVE AFFAIR

There's a danger when reading the Bible that we can be so focused on the words on the pages that we forget to focus on the One who is described by those words. God wants us to do both, to learn more about Him from the stories and writings about Him in the Bible, and then to use those Scriptures to deepen our understanding of and relationship with Him.

1. *Why did Jesus rebuke the religious leaders of His day in John 5:39-40, when they were obviously searching the Scriptures diligently, which would seem like a good thing? What warning is there for us in these words today?*

2. *What might you do differently as a result of reading this warning? What added dimension might this bring to the way you read your Bible from now on?*

THE TOP 100 VERSES IN THE BIBLE

The following list of Bible verses features some of the most famous and best-loved verses in all of Scripture. Each one is excellent for meditation, memorization, or just plain inspiration.

This list was compiled using the actual search results from a popular website called BibleGateway.com, which features a searchable Bible in over 100 versions and 50 languages. The results were based on over 25 million searches made during March and April, 2009, where visitors searched for just one verse at a time. (The earlier portion of this book was based on the search results where visitors looked up larger passages or entire chapters at a time, which resulted in the list of the top 20 passages in the Bible.)

All verses quoted here are taken from *The Holy Bible, New International Version (Copyright © 1973, 1978, 1984),* as they originally appeared in BibleGateway.com's search results.

1. *John 3:16: "For God so loved the world that he gave his one and only Son, that whoever believes in him shall not perish but have eternal life"*

2. *Jeremiah 29:11: "For I know the plans I have for you," declares the LORD, "plans to prosper you and not to harm you, plans to give you hope and a future."*

3. *Romans 8:28: And we know that in all things God works for the good of those who love him, who have been called according to his purpose.*

4. *Philippians 4:13: I can do everything through him who gives me strength.*

5. *Genesis 1:1: In the beginning God created the heavens and the earth.*

6. *Proverbs 3:5: Trust in the LORD with all your heart and lean not on your own understanding...*

7. *Proverbs 3:6: ...in all your ways acknowledge him, and he will make your paths straight.*

8. *Romans 12:2: Do not conform any longer to the pattern of this world, but be transformed by the renewing of your mind. Then you will be able to test and approve what God's will is—his good, pleasing and perfect will.*

9. *Philippians 4:6: Do not be anxious about anything, but in everything, by prayer and petition, with thanksgiving, present your requests to God.*

10. *Matthew 28:19: Therefore go and make disciples of all nations, baptizing them in the name of the Father and of the Son and of the Holy Spirit.*

11. *Ephesians 2:8: For it is by grace you have been saved, through faith—and this not from yourselves, it is the gift of God...*

12. *Galatians 5:22: But the fruit of the Spirit is love, joy, peace, patience, kindness, goodness, faithfulness...*

13. *Romans 12:1: Therefore, I urge you, brothers, in view of God's mercy, to offer your bodies as living sacrifices, holy and pleasing to God—this is your spiritual act of worship.*

14. *John 10:10: The thief comes only to steal and kill and destroy; I have come that they may have life, and have it to the full.*

15. *Acts 18:10: For I am with you, and no one is going to attack and harm you, because I have many people in this city."*

16. *Acts 18:9: One night the Lord spoke to Paul in*

a vision: *"Do not be afraid; keep on speaking, do not be silent."*

17. *Acts 18:11: So Paul stayed for a year and a half, teaching them the word of God.*

18. *Galatians 2:20: I have been crucified with Christ and I no longer live, but Christ lives in me. The life I live in the body, I live by faith in the Son of God, who loved me and gave himself for me.*

19. *1 John 1:9: If we confess our sins, he is faithful and just and will forgive us our sins and purify us from all unrighteousness.*

20. *Romans 3:23: ...for all have sinned and fall short of the glory of God...*

21. *John 14:6: Jesus answered, "I am the way and the truth and the life. No one comes to the Father except through me."*

22. *Matthew 28:20: "...and teaching them to obey everything I have commanded you. And surely I am with you always, to the very end of the age."*

23. *Romans 5:8: But God demonstrates his own love for us in this: While we were still sinners, Christ died for us.*

24. *Philippians 4:8: Finally, brothers, whatever is*

true, whatever is noble, whatever is right, whatever is pure, whatever is lovely, whatever is admirable—if anything is excellent or praiseworthy—think about such things.

25. Philippians 4:7: *And the peace of God, which transcends all understanding, will guard your hearts and your minds in Christ Jesus.*

26. Joshua 1:9: *"Have I not commanded you? Be strong and courageous. Do not be terrified; do not be discouraged, for the LORD your God will be with you wherever you go."*

27. Isaiah 40:31: *...but those who hope in the LORD will renew their strength. They will soar on wings like eagles; they will run and not grow weary, they will walk and not be faint.*

28. Ephesians 2:9: *...not by works, so that no one can boast.*

29. Romans 6:23: *For the wages of sin is death, but the gift of God is eternal life in Christ Jesus our Lord.*

30. Galatians 5:23: *...gentleness and self-control. Against such things there is no law.*

31. Isaiah 53:5: *But he was pierced for our transgres-*

sions, he was crushed for our iniquities; the punishment that brought us peace was upon him, and by his wounds we are healed.

32. 1 Peter 3:15: But in your hearts set apart Christ as Lord. Always be prepared to give an answer to everyone who asks you to give the reason for the hope that you have. But do this with gentleness and respect...

33. 2 Timothy 3:16: All Scripture is God-breathed and is useful for teaching, rebuking, correcting and training in righteousness...

34. Matthew 6:33: But seek first his kingdom and his righteousness, and all these things will be given to you as well.

35. Hebrews 12:2: Let us fix our eyes on Jesus, the author and perfecter of our faith, who for the joy set before him endured the cross, scorning its shame, and sat down at the right hand of the throne of God.

36. 1 Peter 5:7: Cast all your anxiety on him because he cares for you.

37. Ephesians 2:10: For we are God's workmanship, created in Christ Jesus to do good works, which God prepared in advance for us to do.

38. 1 Corinthians 10:13: No temptation has seized you except what is common to man. And God is faithful; he will not let you be tempted beyond what you can bear. But when you are tempted, he will also provide a way out so that you can stand up under it.

39. Matthew 11:28: "Come to me, all you who are weary and burdened, and I will give you rest."

40. Hebrews 11:1: Now faith is being sure of what we hope for and certain of what we do not see.

41. 2 Corinthians 5:17: Therefore, if anyone is in Christ, he is a new creation; the old has gone, the new has come!

42. Hebrews 13:5: Keep your lives free from the love of money and be content with what you have, because God has said, "Never will I leave you; never will I forsake you."

43. 2 Corinthians 12:9: But he said to me, "My grace is sufficient for you, for my power is made perfect in weakness." Therefore I will boast all the more gladly about my weaknesses, so that Christ's power may rest on me.

44. Romans 10:9: That if you confess with your mouth, "Jesus is Lord," and believe in your heart that God raised him from the dead, you will be saved.

45. Isaiah 41:10: So do not fear, for I am with you; do not be dismayed, for I am your God. I will strengthen you and help you; I will uphold you with my righteous right hand.

46. Genesis 1:26: Then God said, "Let us make man in our image, in our likeness, and let them rule over the fish of the sea and the birds of the air, over the livestock, over all the earth, and over all the creatures that move along the ground."

47. Matthew 11:29: "Take my yoke upon you and learn from me, for I am gentle and humble in heart, and you will find rest for your souls."

48. John 16:33: "I have told you these things, so that in me you may have peace. In this world you will have trouble. But take heart! I have overcome the world."

49. Acts 1:8: "But you will receive power when the Holy Spirit comes on you; and you will be my witnesses in Jerusalem, and in all Judea and Samaria, and to the ends of the earth."

50. 2 Timothy 1:7: For God did not give us a spirit

of timidity, but a spirit of power, of love and of self-discipline.

51. Isaiah 53:4: *Surely he took up our infirmities and carried our sorrows, yet we considered him stricken by God, smitten by him, and afflicted.*

52. 2 Corinthians 5:21: *God made him who had no sin to be sin for us, so that in him we might become the righteousness of God.*

53. Romans 15:13: *May the God of hope fill you with all joy and peace as you trust in him, so that you may overflow with hope by the power of the Holy Spirit.*

54. John 11:25: *Jesus said to her, "I am the resurrection and the life. He who believes in me will live, even though he dies..."*

55. Hebrews 11:6: *And without faith it is impossible to please God, because anyone who comes to him must believe that he exists and that he rewards those who earnestly seek him.*

56. John 5:24: *"I tell you the truth, whoever hears my word and believes him who sent me has eternal life and will not be condemned; he has crossed over from death to life."*

57. James 1:2: Consider it pure joy, my brothers, whenever you face trials of many kinds...

58. Isaiah 53:6: We all, like sheep, have gone astray, each of us has turned to his own way; and the LORD has laid on him the iniquity of us all.

59. Acts 2:38: Peter replied, "Repent and be baptized, every one of you, in the name of Jesus Christ for the forgiveness of your sins. And you will receive the gift of the Holy Spirit."

60. Ephesians 3:20: Now to him who is able to do immeasurably more than all we ask or imagine, according to his power that is at work within us...

61. Matthew 11:30: "For my yoke is easy and my burden is light."

62. Genesis 1:27: So God created man in his own image, in the image of God he created him; male and female he created them.

63. Colossians 3:12: Therefore, as God's chosen people, holy and dearly loved, clothe yourselves with compassion, kindness, humility, gentleness and patience.

64. Hebrews 12:1: Therefore, since we are surrounded by such a great cloud of witnesses, let us throw off everything that hinders and the sin that so easily entangles, and let us run with perseverance the race marked out for us.

65. James 5:16: Therefore confess your sins to each other and pray for each other so that you may be healed. The prayer of a righteous man is powerful and effective.

66. Acts 17:11: Now the Bereans were of more noble character than the Thessalonians, for they received the message with great eagerness and examined the Scriptures every day to see if what Paul said was true.

67. Philippians 4:19: And my God will meet all your needs according to his glorious riches in Christ Jesus.

68. John 1:1: In the beginning was the Word, and the Word was with God, and the Word was God.

69. 1 Corinthians 6:19: Do you not know that your body is a temple of the Holy Spirit, who is in you, whom you have received from God? You are not your own;

70. 1 John 3:16: This is how we know what love is: Jesus Christ laid down his life for us. And we ought to lay down our lives for our brothers.

71. *Psalm 133:1: How good and pleasant it is when brothers live together in unity!*

72. *John 14:27: Peace I leave with you; my peace I give you. I do not give to you as the world gives. Do not let your hearts be troubled and do not be afraid.*

73. *Hebrews 4:12: For the word of God is living and active. Sharper than any double-edged sword, it penetrates even to dividing soul and spirit, joints and marrow; it judges the thoughts and attitudes of the heart.*

74. *John 15:13: Greater love has no one than this, that he lay down his life for his friends.*

75. *Micah 6:8: He has showed you, O man, what is good. And what does the LORD require of you? To act justly and to love mercy and to walk humbly with your God.*

76. *Romans 10:17: Consequently, faith comes from hearing the message, and the message is heard through the word of Christ.*

77. *John 1:12: Yet to all who received him, to those who believed in his name, he gave the right to become children of God...*

78. *James 1:12: Blessed is the man who perseveres under trial, because when he has stood the test, he will receive the crown of life that God has promised to those who love him.*

79. *James 1:3: because you know that the testing of your faith develops perseverance.*

80. *Romans 8:38: For I am convinced that neither death nor life, neither angels nor demons, neither the present nor the future, nor any powers...*

81. *Romans 8:39: ...neither height nor depth, nor anything else in all creation, will be able to separate us from the love of God that is in Christ Jesus our Lord.*

82. *Hebrews 10:25: Let us not give up meeting together, as some are in the habit of doing, but let us encourage one another—and all the more as you see the Day approaching.*

83. *2 Peter 1:4: Through these he has given us his very great and precious promises, so that through them you may participate in the divine nature and escape the corruption in the world caused by evil desires.*

84. *Philippians 1:6: ...being confident of this, that he*

who began a good work in you will carry it on to completion until the day of Christ Jesus.

85. *Psalm 133:3: It is as if the dew of Hermon were falling on Mount Zion. For there the LORD bestows his blessing, even life forevermore.*

86. *Hebrews 4:16: Let us then approach the throne of grace with confidence, so that we may receive mercy and find grace to help us in our time of need.*

87. *Psalm 37:4: Delight yourself in the LORD and he will give you the desires of your heart.*

88. *John 3:17: For God did not send his Son into the world to condemn the world, but to save the world through him.*

89. *Acts 4:12: "Salvation is found in no one else, for there is no other name under heaven given to men by which we must be saved."*

90. *Isaiah 26:3: You will keep in perfect peace him whose mind is steadfast, because he trusts in you.*

91. *1 Peter 2:24: He himself bore our sins in his body on the tree, so that we might die to sins and live for righteousness; by his wounds you have been healed.*

92. *Joshua 1:8: Do not let this Book of the Law depart from your mouth; meditate on it day and night, so that you may be careful to do everything written in it. Then you will be prosperous and successful.*

93. *Matt 28:18: Then Jesus came to them and said, "All authority in heaven and on earth has been given to me."*

94. *Colossians 3:23: Whatever you do, work at it with all your heart, as working for the Lord, not for men...*

95. *Matthew 22:37: Jesus replied: "Love the Lord your God with all your heart and with all your soul and with all your mind."*

96. *Psalm 133:2: It is like precious oil poured on the head, running down on the beard, running down on Aaron's beard, down upon the collar of his robes.*

97. *Matthew 5:16: In the same way, let your light shine before men, that they may see your good deeds and praise your Father in heaven.*

98. *Isaiah 55:8: "For my thoughts are not your thoughts, neither are your ways my ways," declares the LORD.*

99. *Hebrews 4:15: For we do not have a high priest who is unable to sympathize with our weaknesses, but we have one who has been tempted in every way, just as we are—yet was without sin.*

100. *John 13:35: "By this all men will know that you are my disciples, if you love one another."*

About The Author

Described by *USA Today* as "a new breed of evangelist," Eric Elder is an ordained pastor, songwriter and the creator of *The Ranch,* a faith-boosting website that attracts thousands of visitors each month at www.TheRanch.org.

Eric is also an inspirational writer and speaker, having written about spiritual issues for publications like Billy Graham's *Decision Magazine,* and spoken about faith at national conferences like the Exodus International *Freedom Conference.*

If you've enjoyed this book, you may enjoy some of Eric's other writings, including: *Two Weeks With God, Exodus: Lessons In Freedom, Jesus: Lessons In Love, Nehemiah: Lessons In Rebuilding, Ephesians: Lessons In Grace, Acts: Lessons In Faith, Israel: Lessons From The Holy Land,* and *What God Says About Sex.*

To listen to, download or order more inspiring resources like these, please visit:

www.TheRanch.org

Printed in Great Britain
by Amazon.co.uk, Ltd.,
Marston Gate.